The Royal Line of Succession

OFFICIAL SOUVENIR GUIDE

HUGO VICKERS

SI IVVAT HEROVM CLARAS VIDISSE FIGVRAS,
SPECTA HAS MAIORES NVLLA TABELLA TVLIT,
CERTAMEN MAGNVM LIS QVÆSTIO MAGNA PATERNE,
FILIVS AN VINCAT VICIT VTERQVE QVIDEM ·
ISTE SVOS HOSTES PATRIÆQVE INCENDIA SÆPE
SVSTVLIT ET PACEM CIVIBVS VSQVE DEDIT ·

FILIVS AD MAIORA QVIDEM PROGNATVS AB ARIS
SVBMOVET INDIGNOS SVESTITVTQVE PROBOS ·
CERTÆ VIRTVTI PAPARVM AVDACIA CESSIT,
HENRICO OCTAVO SCEPTRA GERENTE MANV ·
REDDITA RELIGIO EST ISTO REGNANTE DEIQVE
DOGMATA CEPERVNT ESSE IN HONORE SVO ·

PROTOTYPVM IVSTÆ MAGNITVDINIS IPSO OPERE TECTORIO
FECIT HOLBENIVS IVBENTE HENRICO · VIII ·
ECTYPVM A REMIGIO VAN LEEMPVT BREVIORI TABELLA
DESCRIBI VOLVIT   CAROLVS · II · M · B · F · E · H · R ·
A° · DNI · MDCLXVII ·

Contents

ORDER OF SUCCESSION

This book shows the royal line of succession. Sons take precedence over daughters in the order of succession, so they have been listed first in the main genealogical family trees, regardless of actual order of birth.

OPPOSITE
Remigius van Leemput (1607–75), *Henry VIII, Henry VII, Elizabeth of York and Jane Seymour*, 1667, after original by Hans Holbein the Younger (1497/8–1543), 1537.

RIGHT
Sir Anthony Van Dyck (1599–1641), *The five eldest children of Charles I*, 1637.

Find out more about the Royal Collection at **www.royalcollection.org.uk**

Introduction

RIGHT
Marcus Adams
(1875–1959),
*The Royal Family,
including Dookie, at
Buckingham Palace,*
20 December 1938.

BELOW
Cecil Beaton (1904–80),
*King George VI and
Queen Elizabeth with
Princesses Elizabeth
and Margaret,*
November 1943.

The United Kingdom has a hereditary monarchy, whereby the Crown passes by succession from one sovereign to another. The system is based on the rules of the inheritance of land, and on primogeniture, according to which, if there is a direct male heir, he takes precedence over the females of the family. If the sovereign has a daughter, but no son, she takes precedence over other male members of the family. Thus Queen Elizabeth II succeeded to the throne because her father, King George VI, had no son and she was his elder daughter.

Fitness to rule was also a consideration from the earliest days of the English monarchy, when the reigning king often bypassed his immediate successor in favour of a more suitable candidate who could provide leadership. Two other elements that have been incorporated over the centuries are the statutory principle and the elective principle. In Anglo-Saxon times, the Witan (a council composed of members of the ruling class) elected the king – the elective principle. The last vestige of this is the Recognition at the beginning of the coronation service, when the Archbishop of Canterbury presents the new monarch to the assembled people for their acclamation. The element of statute was established in the Bill of Rights of 1689, and was strengthened by the Act of Settlement in 1701 (for details of both, see pages 36 and 37). The British monarchy today is thus both hereditary and constitutional.

Subject to the Bill of Rights, a new sovereign succeeds to the throne automatically. However, the sovereign will not be anointed and crowned, and thus acknowledged as king or queen, without speaking and signing the Declaration prescribed by Act of Parliament, and making the coronation oath at the coronation service. The Declaration is normally made in the House of Lords, in the presence of the two Houses of Parliament, at the first State Opening of Parliament of the new reign. If there is no Opening of Parliament before the coronation (as happened in 1937), the Archbishop of Canterbury administers the Declaration at the beginning of the coronation ceremony.

The Act of Settlement ensured that a Roman Catholic could not become sovereign, and that the sovereign could not be married to a Roman Catholic. The sovereign is obliged to be in communion with the Church of England, and to preserve the established Church of England and the established Church of Scotland. In the accession declaration, he or she must

promise to uphold the Protestant succession.

At the 2011 Commonwealth Heads of Government meeting in Perth, Australia, all the leaders of the Commonwealth realms agreed to introduce legislation to end male primogeniture in relation to succeeding to the throne. This would only affect the descendants of the present Prince of Wales. The new legislation would also allow heirs to the throne to marry Roman Catholics, but the sovereign would still have to be in communion with the Church of England.

The royal line of succession is now well established, but this was not always the case. The family trees in this book trace 2,000 years of the sometimes troubled histories of those men and women who, by accident of birth, found themselves in line to reign.

Pre-Conquest Kings

There are said to have been 24 generations of Saxon chieftains preceding Cerdic, King of Wessex (r.519–34), the Saxon invader who reputedly founded his own kingdom, after arriving in England in AD 495. These genealogies, which may have some accuracy, were passed down orally and eventually listed in the ninth-century Anglo-Saxon Chronicle. Successors to Cerdic ruled not merely by descent; the early kings of Wessex also had to prove their fitness to rule.

By AD 650, the British Isles comprised a number of territories, some ruled by native kings, some ruled by the immigrant Angles, Saxons and Jutes who had invaded southern Britain during the fifth century. It was a period of great struggle for survival, as well as for supremacy. In essence, these rulers were tribal chieftains, later described by Latin writers as *reges*, or kings.

Their kingdoms came to be known as the Heptarchy, or the rule of seven: Bernicia, Deira, Lindsey, East Anglia, Mercia, Wessex and Kent; these evolved into Northumbria (formed when Bernicia and Deira joined in AD 651), Essex, East Anglia, Mercia, Wessex, Sussex and Kent. The lineage of Cerdic of Wessex is most often credited with having laid the foundations of the British monarchy.

The Venerable Bede (672–735), who chronicled the early history of England in his *Ecclesiastical History of the English People*, identified a further seven warrior kings as important figures. Of these, Ceawlin (r.560–91) and Ine (r.688–726) were of particular importance – Ceawlin for his part in the expansion of Anglo-Saxon territory, and Ine for his role in the advancement of Christianity in the kingdom of Wessex.

Cynegils (r.611–43) was one of the first kings to embrace the Christian faith; while both Caedwalla (r.685–8) and Ine abdicated in order to make pilgrimages to Rome.

In the ninth century, Egbert, King of Wessex (r.802–39), founded a united England by subduing the various other kingdoms, and was pronounced 'King of the English'. However, it was during this period that Britain faced a series of invasions from Denmark and the prospect of Viking kings on the English throne.

Sceaf — **Heremod** — **Godwulf** — **Woden** — **Freawine**

Bedwig — **Sceldwa** — **Finn** — **Baeldaeg** — **Wig**

Hwala — **Beaw** — **Frithuwulf** — **Brand (Brond?)** — **Gewis**

Hathra — **Taetwa** — **Frealaf** — **Frithugar (Frithogar?)** — **Esla (Elsa?)**

Itermon — **Geata** — **Frithuwald** — **Elesa**

CERDIC
KING OF WESSEX
r.519–34

CYNRIC
KING OF WESSEX
r.534–60

A sister

CEAWLIN
KING OF WESSEX
r.560–91
(deposed by Ceol/Ceolric; d.593)

Cutha
(d.584 in Battle of Fethanleag)

Cuthwulf
(d.571)

Cwichelm(?)
(d.593)

Stuf

Wihtgar
King of the Isle of Wight
(d.544, ancestor of King Alfred the Great)

Cuthwine

CEOL
(or CEOLRIC)
KING OF WESSEX
r.591–7

CEOLWULF
KING OF WESSEX
r.597–611

CYNEGILS
KING OF WESSEX
r.611–43

Cynebald

Cedda

Cutha

Cuthgils

Ethelbald

Coenberht
(d.661)

Ceolwald

Cwichelm
(d.636)

CENWALH
KING OF WESSEX
r.643–72
= (1) a sister of Penda King of Mercia (m. repudiated 645)
= (2) SEAXBURH QUEEN OF WESSEX r.672–4
(d. or deposed 674)

CENTWINE
KING OF WESSEX
r.676–85
(probably killed by his kinsman, Caedwalla)
=
a sister of Eormenurh (2nd wife of Ecgfrith, King of Northumbria)

Cyneburg(?)
= c.635
St Oswald
King of Northumbria
(d.641 in Battle of Oswestry)

St Eglewine
(or Ethelwine)

Cenferth

Oswald
(d.730)

CAEDWALLA
(c.659–89)
KING OF WESSEX
r.685–8
(abdicated)

Mul
(burned to death 687)

Cenred

Cuthred
(d.661)

Bugge

CENFUS
KING OF WESSEX
r.674

ETHELHEARD
KING OF WESSEX
r.726–40
=
Frithugyth

Ethelburh
(sister of Ethelheard)
=

INE
KING OF WESSEX
r.688–726
(abdicated; d. post 726)

Ingild
(d.718)

Cwenburh

Cuthburh
=
Aldfrith
King of Northumbria
(d.705)

AESCWINE
KING OF WESSEX
r.674–6

Eoppa

Eafa

Ealhmund

EGBERT
(c.770/75–839)
KING OF ENGLAND
KING OF WESSEX r.802–39
KING OF KENT, SURREY, SUSSEX, ESSEX & EAST ANGLIA r.825–39
KING OF MERCIA r.829–39
(see KINGS OF ALL ENGLAND)

ABBREVIATIONS

b.	born
c.	circa (about)
d.	died
diss.	dissolved
div.	divorced
k.	killed
m.	marriage
r.	reigned
=	married
≠	not married

RECORDED AS KINGS, BUT OF UNKNOWN GENEALOGY

CUTHRED
KING OF WESSEX
r.740–56

Cynric

SIGEBERHT
KING OF WESSEX
r.756–7
(deposed by Cynewulf; stabbed by a herdsman near Peterborough, post 757)

CYNEWULF
KING OF WESSEX
r.757–86
(killed by Sigeberht's brother Cyneheard)

BEORHTRIC
KING OF WESSEX
r.786–802
(accidentally poisoned by his wife, 802)
= 789
Eadburh
daughter of Offa, King of Mercia

Ethelheard (and his sister Ethelburh), Cuthred, Sigeberht and Beorhtric were all said to be 'of the lineage of Cerdic'.

Kings of All England

Around 799, Egbert was driven into exile by Beorhtric, King of Wessex (r.786–802). Egbert returned to England as King of the West Saxons, and in 802 subdued Cornwall, defeated the King of Mercia and annexed Kent, becoming overlord of all the English kings in 829.

On his death in 839, Egbert was succeeded by his son, Ethelwulf (r.839–55), most of whose reign was spent repelling raids by the Danes. After the death of his first wife, Ethelwulf made a pilgrimage to Rome, and on his return through France he married Judith, daughter of Charles II (the Bald), King of France (823–77). This established a strong bond against the Vikings with the most powerful country in Christendom. When Ethelwulf died, his son Ethelbald (r.855–60) married his widowed stepmother, perhaps to try to preserve this alliance. After Ethelbald's death, three of his brothers reigned in succession, one of whom, Ethelred I (r.866–71), fought in six battles against the Danes, eventually dying of wounds sustained at the battle of Merton.

The youngest brother was Alfred the Great (r.871–99), who also spent his reign fighting the Danes. In 878 he was forced to retreat to Athelney in Somerset, where, preoccupied with military strategy, he famously 'burnt the cakes' he had been asked to watch by a herdsman's wife. However, he managed to hold Wessex, took London in 886, and went on to build a large fleet and an army for his kingdom. He imposed a strong sense of regal authority and Christian morality on his people, introduced codes of law and religious and educational reforms, and greatly strengthened the position of the monarchy.

Alfred was succeeded by his son, Edward I (the Elder) (r.899–924), though the succession was disputed by Edward's cousin, Ethelwold, son of Ethelred I. Edward subdued the Welsh and ruled as far north as the Humber. His overlordship was recognised by some of the kings of Northumbria and Scotland. He was succeeded by his son, Athelstan (r.924–39), who extended his overlordship even further into the kingdoms of York and Scotland;

it is said that he never lost a battle. Athelstan was respected by foreign kings, bishops and nobles, and forged alliances by marrying four of his half-sisters to European rulers.

Athelstan died, unmarried, in 939, and was succeeded by his half-brother, Edmund I (the Magnificent) (r.939–46). Edmund I seized control of many towns from the Danes, including Leicester and Derby. He also forged an alliance with Malcolm I, King of the Scots (d.954), by handing over Northumbria and Strathclyde. Edmund was killed in the course of a struggle with an intruder at Pucklechurch, Gloucestershire, in 946, and was succeeded by his brother, Edred (r.946–55), as his own sons were too young to rule.

On Edred's death, Edmund's son, Edwy the Fair (r.955–9), became King. Edwy's untimely death meant that his brother, Edgar the Peaceful (r.959–75), succeeded him. Edgar's authority extended to Ireland and his was a largely peaceful reign, during which he helped to establish the English monastic system with Dunstan, Archbishop of Canterbury.

Edward II (the Martyr) (r.975–9) was Edgar's son by his first marriage. His succession to the throne was disputed by his stepmother, Elfrida (c.945–1000), who wanted to see her own son, Ethelred, crowned. Edward was murdered, in 979, while on a hunting trip, on Elfrida's orders.

Ethelred II (r.979–1013, 1014–16) was a mere boy when he became King, earning him the nickname 'the Unready' or 'the Redeless', since he was deemed unable to discern good counsel, or rede. He struggled to fend off Danish raids and eventually instituted the Danegeld, a regular payment to buy off the Danes. After Ethelred ordered a massacre of all Danes in England, in 1003,

a period of further attacks and invasions ensued, and Ethelred lost the throne to Sweyn Forkbeard, King of Denmark, in 1013. Ethelred fled to Normandy.

Sweyn was the son of Harold Bluetooth, King of Denmark (d.986). He had made various conquests in Sweden and Norway, and his raids on Britain began in 991. Having ousted Ethelred II to become the first Danish King of England (r.1013–14), he died the following year, and the throne reverted to Ethelred.

BELOW
J. Stratford, sketched from a sculpture by A.W. Warren, *Canute the Great, King of England, Denmark and Norway,* 1804. Canute provided firm and effective government for these countries during his reign.

CANUTE THE GREAT

Kings of All England

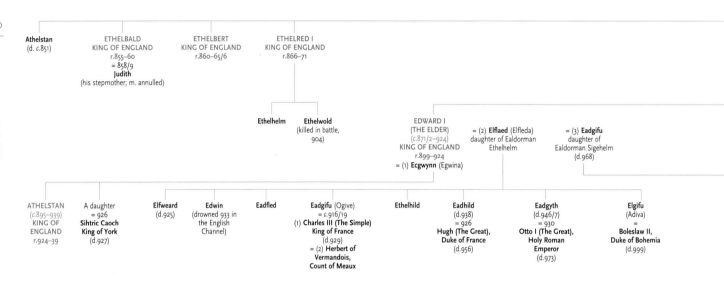

EGBERT
(c.770/75–839)
KING OF ENGLAND
KING OF WESSEX r.802–39
KING OF KENT, SURREY, SUSSEX, ESSEX & EAST ANGLIA r.825–39
KING OF MERCIA r.829–39

Athelstan
(d. *c.*851)

ETHELBALD
KING OF ENGLAND
r.855–60
= 858/9
Judith
(his stepmother; m. annulled)

ETHELBERT
KING OF ENGLAND
r.860–65/6

ETHELRED I
KING OF ENGLAND
r.866–71

Ethelhelm

Ethelwold
(killed in battle,
904)

EDWARD I
(THE ELDER)
(c.871/2–924)
KING OF ENGLAND
r.899–924
= (1) **Ecgwynn** (Egwina)

= (2) **Elflaed** (Elfleda)
daughter of Ealdorman
Ethelhelm

= (3) **Eadgifu**
daughter of
Ealdorman Sigehelm
(d.968)

ATHELSTAN
(c.895–939)
KING OF
ENGLAND
r.924–39

A daughter
= 926
Sihtric Caoch
King of York
(d.927)

Elfweard
(d.925)

Edwin
(drowned 933 in
the English
Channel)

Eadfled

Eadgifu (Ogive)
= *c.*916/19
(1) **Charles III (The Simple)**
King of France
(d.929)
= (2) **Herbert of**
Vermandois,
Count of Meaux

Ethelhild

Eadhild
(d.938)
= 926
Hugh (The Great),
Duke of France
(d.956)

Eadgyth
(d.946/7)
= 930
Otto I (The Great),
Holy Roman
Emperor
(d.973)

Elgifu
(Adiva)
=
Boleslaw II,
Duke of Bohemia
(d.999)

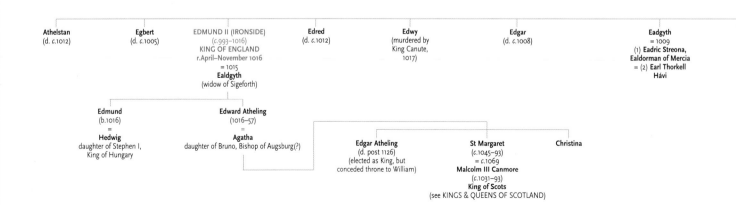

Athelstan
(d. *c.*1012)

Egbert
(d. *c.*1005)

EDMUND II (IRONSIDE)
(c.993–1016)
KING OF ENGLAND
r.April–November 1016
= 1015
Ealdgyth
(widow of Sigeforth)

Edred
(d. *c.*1012)

Edwy
(murdered by
King Canute,
1017)

Edgar
(d. *c.*1008)

Eadgyth
= 1009
(1) **Eadric Streona,**
Ealdorman of Mercia
= (2) **Earl Thorkell**
Hávi

Edmund
(b.1016)
=
Hedwig
daughter of Stephen I,
King of Hungary

Edward Atheling
(1016–57)
=
Agatha
daughter of Bruno, Bishop of Augsburg(?)

Edgar Atheling
(d. post 1126)
(elected as King, but
conceded throne to William)

St Margaret
*(c.*1045–93)
= *c.*1069
Malcolm III Canmore
*(c.*1031–93)
King of Scots
(see KINGS & QUEENS OF SCOTLAND)

Christina

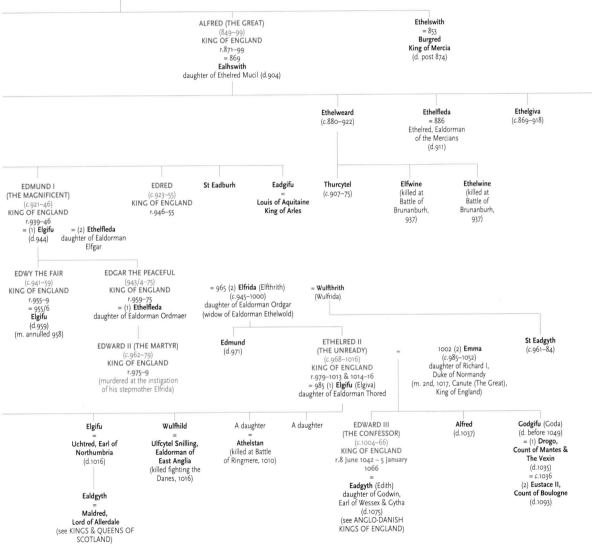

ATHELING
Atheling is a title given to a royal prince, deriving from the Old English *aethelu* (noble family).

EALDORMAN
Ealdorman is an official appointed by a king to be responsible for law, order and justice in a shire and to lead his local militia in battle. Later replaced by earl, the title derives from the Old English *ealdor* (lord).

ETHELWULF
(c.795/800–858)
KING OF ENGLAND
r.839–55 (abdicated)
= (1) **Osburh**
daughter of Ealdorman Oslac, descendant of Wihtgar, nephew of Cynric (d. c.853)

= 856 (2) **Judith**
(b. c.844?)
daughter of Charles II (The Bald), King of France & Holy Roman Emperor,
m. 2nd, 858/9, King Ethelbald, her stepson (m. annulled),
m. 3rd, 863, Baldwin I, Count of Flanders (d.879)

ALFRED (THE GREAT)
(849–99)
KING OF ENGLAND
r.871–99
= 869
Ealhswith
daughter of Ethelred Mucil (d.904)

Ethelswith
= 853
Burgred
King of Mercia
(d. post 874)

Ethelweard
(c.880–922)

Ethelfleda
= 886
Ethelred, Ealdorman
of the Mercians
(d.911)

Ethelgiva
(c.869–918)

Elfthryth
(Elftrudis)
(c.877–c.929)
= c.893/9
Baldwin II (The Bald), Count of Flanders
(c.864–918)
son of Baldwin I & Judith, widow of
King Ethelwulf & ex-wife of King Ethelbald

EDMUND I
(THE MAGNIFICENT)
(c.921–46)
KING OF ENGLAND
r.939–46
= (1) **Elgifu**
(d.944)
= (2) **Ethelfleda**
daughter of Ealdorman
Elfgar

EDRED
(c.923–55)
KING OF ENGLAND
r.946–55

St Eadburh

Eadgifu
=
Louis of Aquitaine
King of Arles

Thurcytel
(c.907–75)

Elfwine
(killed at
Battle of
Brunanburh,
937)

Ethelwine
(killed at
Battle of
Brunanburh,
937)

Arnold I
Count of Flanders
(c.889–964)
=
Adaele de Vermandois
(c.910–60)

Baldwin III
(c.933–62)
=
Matilde,
Princess of Saxony
(c.937–1008)

EDWY THE FAIR
(c.941–59)
KING OF ENGLAND
r.955–9
=
Elgifu
(d.959)
(m. annulled 958)

EDGAR THE PEACEFUL
(943/4–75)
KING OF ENGLAND
r.959–75
= (1) **Ethelfleda**
daughter of Ealdorman Ordmaer

= 965 (2) **Elfrida** (Elfthrith)
(c.945–1000)
daughter of Ealdorman Ordgar
(widow of Ealdorman Ethelwold)

= **Wulfthrith**
(Wulfrida)

Arnold II
Count of Flanders
(d.987)
=
Roselle, Princess of Italy
(c.945–1003)

EDWARD II (THE MARTYR)
(c.962–79)
KING OF ENGLAND
r.975–9
(murdered at the instigation
of his stepmother Elfrida)

Edmund
(d.971)

ETHELRED II
(THE UNREADY)
(c.968–1016)
KING OF ENGLAND
r.979–1013 & 1014–16
= 985 (1) **Elgifu** (Elgiva)
daughter of Ealdorman Thored

=

1002 (2) **Emma**
(c.985–1052)
daughter of Richard I,
Duke of Normandy
(m. 2nd, 1017, Canute (The Great),
King of England)

St Eadgyth
(c.961–84)

Baldwin IV
Count of Flanders
(c.967–1036/9)
= c.1004
Otgive of Luxembourg
(c.986–1030)

Baldwin V
Count of Flanders,
Regent of France
(c.1012–67)
=
Adele, Princess of France
(c.1003–97)

Elgifu
=
Uchtred, Earl of
Northumbria
(d.1016)

Wulfhild
=
Ulfcytel Snilling,
Ealdorman of
East Anglia
(killed fighting the
Danes, 1016)

A daughter
=
Athelstan
(killed at Battle
of Ringmere, 1010)

A daughter

EDWARD III
(THE CONFESSOR)
(c.1004–66)
KING OF ENGLAND
r.8 June 1042 – 5 January
1066
=
Eadgyth (Edith)
daughter of Godwin,
Earl of Wessex & Gytha
(d.1075)
(see ANGLO-DANISH
KINGS OF ENGLAND)

Alfred
(d.1037)

Godgifu (Goda)
(d. before 1049)
= (1) **Drogo**,
Count of Mantes &
The Vexin
(d.1035)
= c.1036
(2) **Eustace II**,
Count of Boulogne
(d.1093)

Matilda
(c.1031–83)
= c.1051
WILLIAM I
(1027/8–87)
KING OF ENGLAND
(see FAMILY OF WILLIAM THE
CONQUEROR)

Ealdgyth
=
Maldred,
Lord of Allerdale
(see KINGS & QUEENS OF
SCOTLAND)

Ethelred's son, Edmund II (r.April–November 1016), succeeded him. He spent his short reign in continual warfare, and his bravery earned him the nickname 'Ironside'. After being defeated by Canute, son of Sweyn, at Ashington in Essex, Edmund agreed to divide the kingdom with Canute. But Edmund died in 1016, and Canute became sole ruler (r.1016–35).

Canute did not treat England as a conquered country, but divided it into five earldoms, or provinces. Although ruthless in the methods used to establish his position (he carried out a series of assassinations to prevent any threat to his succession, and even married, as his second wife, the widow of Ethelred to secure his line), he proved to be an exceptionally capable and respected ruler.

Canute was succeeded by two sons from his two marriages, who reigned jointly for two years: Harold I (Harefoot) and

Hardicanute (r.1035–7). Harold, son of Elfgiva of Northampton, was King of the district north of the Thames. Hardicanute spent most of his time in Denmark, so Harold was made sole King of England in 1037, and reigned until his death in 1040. Hardicanute was sole King from 1040 until his death in 1042.

During the long conflict with the Danes, the English throne had twice been lost to Danish kings, but in 1042, the English royal family was restored with the succession of Edward III (the Confessor) (r.1042–66), half-brother of Edmund II and also of Canute's son, Hardicanute.

In January 1066, Edward, a venerable and deeply pious man, died, childless. The Witan elected his brother-in-law, Harold Godwinson – son of the all-powerful Godwin, Earl of Wessex (d.1053) – as King Harold II (r.January–October 1066).

Harold II had to cope with contenders to the throne from all sides. William, Duke of Normandy, declared that Edward the Confessor had promised the crown to him, and that Harold had sworn to aid William's accession to the throne when held captive in Normandy in 1053. A further claim came from the King of Norway. Harold II won a victory over the Norwegians at Stamford Bridge, near York, on 25 September 1066, but was killed in battle against William at Hastings, on 14 October.

In 1066, after the death of Harold II, Edgar Atheling, a grandson of Edmund II, was briefly elected King by the English, but conceded the crown to the Norman William the Conqueror. Edgar, the last in the family line of Cerdic, died some time after 1126.

Anglo-Danish Kings of England

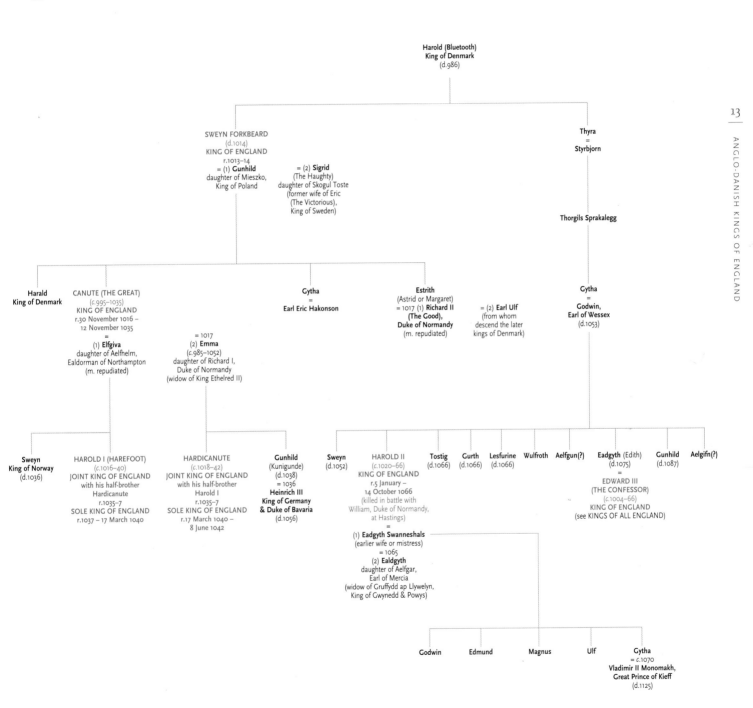

Harold (Bluetooth)
King of Denmark
(d.986)

SWEYN FORKBEARD
(d.1014)
KING OF ENGLAND
r.1013–14
= (1) **Gunhild**
daughter of Mieszko,
King of Poland

= (2) **Sigrid**
(The Haughty)
daughter of Skogul Toste
(former wife of Eric
(The Victorious),
King of Sweden)

Thyra
=
Styrbjorn

Thorgils Sprakalegg

Harald
King of Denmark

CANUTE (THE GREAT)
(c.995–1035)
KING OF ENGLAND
r.30 November 1016 –
12 November 1035
=
(1) **Elfgiva**
daughter of Aelfhelm,
Ealdorman of Northampton
(m. repudiated)

= 1017
(2) **Emma**
(c.985–1052)
daughter of Richard I,
Duke of Normandy
(widow of King Ethelred II)

Gytha
=
Earl Eric Hakonson

Estrith
(Astrid or Margaret)
= 1017 (1) **Richard II**
(**The Good**),
Duke of Normandy
(m. repudiated)

= (2) **Earl Ulf**
(from whom
descend the later
kings of Denmark)

Gytha
=
Godwin,
Earl of Wessex
(d.1053)

Sweyn
King of Norway
(d.1036)

HAROLD I (HAREFOOT)
(c.1016–40)
JOINT KING OF ENGLAND
with his half-brother
Hardicanute
r.1035–7
SOLE KING OF ENGLAND
r.1037 – 17 March 1040

HARDICANUTE
(c.1018–42)
JOINT KING OF ENGLAND
with his half-brother
Harold I
r.1035–7
SOLE KING OF ENGLAND
r.17 March 1040 –
8 June 1042

Gunhild
(Kunigunde)
(d.1038)
= 1036
Heinrich III
King of Germany
& Duke of Bavaria
(d.1056)

Sweyn
(d.1052)

HAROLD II
(c.1020–66)
KING OF ENGLAND
r.5 January –
14 October 1066
(killed in battle with
William, Duke of Normandy,
at Hastings)
=
(1) **Eadgyth Swanneshals**
(earlier wife or mistress)
= 1065
(2) **Ealdgyth**
daughter of Aelfgar,
Earl of Mercia
(widow of Gruffydd ap Llywelyn,
King of Gwynedd & Powys)

Tostig
(d.1066)

Gurth
(d.1066)

Lesfurine
(d.1066)

Wulfroth

Aelfgun(?)

Eadgyth (Edith)
(d.1075)
=
EDWARD III
(THE CONFESSOR)
(c.1004–66)
KING OF ENGLAND
(see KINGS OF ALL ENGLAND)

Gunhild
(d.1087)

Aelgifn(?)

Godwin

Edmund

Magnus

Ulf

Gytha
= c.1070
Vladimir II Monomakh,
Great Prince of Kieff
(d.1125)

Family of William the Conqueror

Following his victory at the Battle of Hastings, William I (r.1066–87) was crowned King of England at Westminster Abbey on Christmas Day 1066. William's claim to the throne was derived from personal and political links, and he obtained papal approval to invade England. His wife, Matilda (c.1031–83), was a direct descendant of Alfred the Great. Most importantly, Edward the Confessor had promised him the succession, c.1051. He reigned wisely, and is credited with the introduction of a system of centralised feudalism. He instigated a survey of England, known to us as the Domesday Book.

William's eldest son, Robert, Duke of Normandy (c.1051/4–1134), rebelled against him and wounded him in single combat in 1079. Although they were reconciled, Robert remained a problem for his father, and William passed over him in the succession. William's second son, Richard (c.1055–81), predeceased him, having been killed while on a hunting trip in the New Forest, and William designated his third son, William Rufus, as his heir.

Known as 'Rufus' or 'the Red King', William II (r.1087–1100), his father's favourite son, was crowned in 1087. He proved to be unpopular, especially with the Church, because of his opposition to reform and his appropriation of Church revenues for his own use. He never married and was killed in mysterious circumstances, while hunting in the New Forest.

William II's younger brother, Henry I

ROYAL TITLES: THE DUKE OF KENT

The title of Earl of Kent was conferred on Odo, Bishop of Bayeux, by his half-brother, William I, and has been recreated several times since. A dukedom of this name was held by the non-royal Henry Grey, from 1710 to 1740. Queen Victoria's father held the title until his death, in 1820. Queen Victoria gave it as an earldom to her second son, Prince Alfred, Duke of Edinburgh, and it became a dukedom once more when conferred on Prince George, fourth son of King George V. It is currently held by Prince George's elder son, Prince Edward.

RIGHT
George Vertue (1684–1756), *William I*. Engraving. Vertue created a series of historical 'portraits' of kings of England, published in London c.1736.

RIGHT
George Vertue,
King Stephen. Engraving.

on the throne, quelling insurrections by opponents and warring with the Scots. His cousin, Matilda, had not given up her claim to the throne, and was set to do battle with Stephen in 1139. In 1141, Stephen was captured, although he was freed by his supporters. Civil wars and the struggle for the throne continued for 12 years. In 1148, Matilda left the country; in 1153, her son, Henry, who had taken her place as claimant to the throne, agreed at the Treaty of Winchester to leave Stephen unmolested, as long as he succeeded the King on his death. In 1154, Henry became King, and the royal lineage took another turn, as Britain entered the era of the great House of Plantagenet.

(Beauclerc) (r.1100–35), secured the throne. Henry married Matilda (1079–1118), daughter of Malcolm III, King of the Scots (c.1031–93), thereby securing the friendship of Scotland. Like his father and brother before him, Henry had to deal with his troublesome brother, Robert, when the subjects of Robert's duchy, weary of their ruler's incompetence, asked Henry to intercede on their behalf. Robert was captured and subsequently died in prison.

Henry I reigned for 35 years; he was known as 'the lion of justice' and as a good diplomat. His two sons, William and Richard, were drowned in 1120, while crossing the Channel near Barfleur, Normandy, and Henry's daughter, Matilda, was declared the heiress presumptive. But on Henry I's death, the crown was claimed by his nephew, Stephen of Blois, who had gathered support among the citizens of London, despite the fact that he had sworn to help Matilda succeed her father.

Stephen (r.1135–54) faced a difficult period

BELOW
George Vertue, *Henry I*.
Engraving.

Family of William the Conqueror

WILLIAM I
(THE CONQUEROR)
(1027/8–87)
KING OF ENGLAND
r.14 October 1066 – 9 September 1087
illegitimate son of Robert le Diable,
Duke of Normandy (Robert I,
'The Magnificent'), and Herlève,
daughter of 'The Tanner', of Falaise

= *c.*1051

Matilda
(*c.*1031–83)
QUEEN MATILDA
daughter of Baldwin V, Count of
Flanders, Regent of France
(direct descendant of
King Alfred the Great)
(see KINGS OF ALL ENGLAND)

Robert II (Curthose)
Duke of Normandy
(*c.*1051/4–1134)
= 1100
Sibylla
(d.1103)
daughter of Geoffrey,
Count of Conservano

Richard
(*c.*1055–81)
(killed while hunting
in the New Forest)

WILLIAM II
(RUFUS)
(*c.*1055/60–1100)
KING OF ENGLAND
r.9 September 1087 –
2 August 1100
(killed while hunting
in the New Forest)

HENRY I
(HENRY BEAUCLERC)
(1068–1135)
KING OF ENGLAND
r.2 August 1100 – 1 December 1135
= 1100
(1) **Matilda** (Edith)
(1079–1118)
QUEEN MATILDA
daughter of Malcolm III, King of
Scots & great-granddaughter of
King Edmund II

= 1121 (2) **Adeliza**
(*c.*1104–51)
QUEEN ADELIZA
daughter of Godfrey I
(The Bearded),
Duke of Lower Lorraine
(m. 2nd, 1138, William
d'Aubigny,
1st Earl of Arundel
(d.1176))

William Clito,
Count of Flanders
(1101–28)
(died of a wound received at
St Omer)
= 1123 (1) **Sibylla**
(1112–65)
daughter of Fulk V,
Count of Anjou & Maine,
and sister of Geoffrey V,
(m. annulled 1124)
(m. 2nd, 1134,
Thierry of Alsace, Count of Flanders)
= 1128 (2) **Joan**
daughter of Guillaume I,
Count of Burgundy
(ex-wife of Louis VI,
King of France, and widow of
Umberto II, Count of Savoy)

Henry
(b.1102)
(killed while hunting
in the New Forest)

William the Atheling,
Duke of Normandy
(1103–20)
(drowned off Barfleur,
Normandy)
= 1119
Matilda (Alice)
(1107–54)
daughter of Fulk V,
Count of Anjou & Maine,
and sister of Geoffrey V

Richard
(d.1120)
(drowned off Barfleur,
Normandy)

Matilda
Heiress Presumptive
(*c.*1102–67)
= 1114
(1) **Heinrich V**
King of Germany,
Holy Roman Emperor
(d.1125)
= 1127 (2) **Geoffrey V,**
Count of Anjou & Maine
(1113–51)
brother of Matilda,
Duchess of Normandy

HENRY II
(CURTMANTLE)
(1133–89)
KING OF ENGLAND
(see HOUSE OF
PLANTAGENET)

Geoffrey VI Martel,
Count of Nantes
(1134–58)

William
(1136–64)

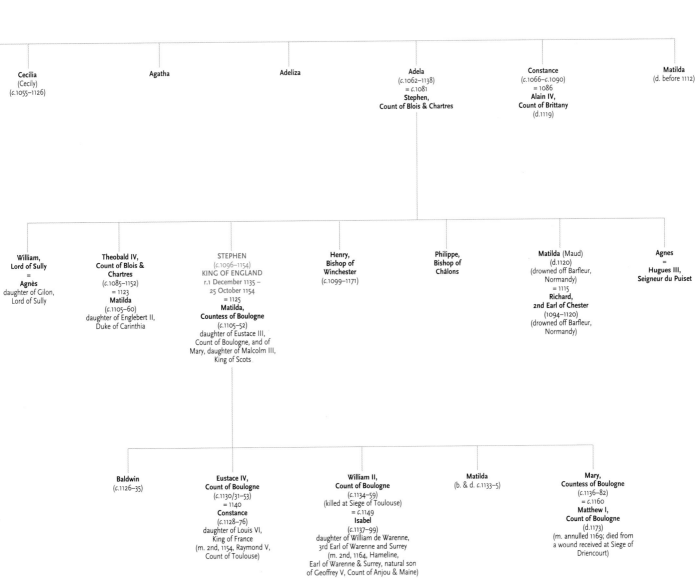

Cecilia
(Cecily)
(c.1055–1126)

Agatha

Adeliza

Adela
(c.1062–1138)
= c.1081
Stephen,
Count of Blois & Chartres

Constance
(c.1066–c.1090)
= 1086
Alain IV,
Count of Brittany
(d.1119)

Matilda
(d. before 1112)

William,
Lord of Sully
=
Agnès
daughter of Gilon,
Lord of Sully

Theobald IV,
Count of Blois &
Chartres
(c.1085–1152)
= 1123
Matilda
(c.1105–60)
daughter of Englebert II,
Duke of Carinthia

STEPHEN
(c.1096–1154)
KING OF ENGLAND
r.1 December 1135 –
25 October 1154
= 1125
Matilda,
Countess of Boulogne
(c.1105–52)
daughter of Eustace III,
Count of Boulogne, and of
Mary, daughter of Malcolm III,
King of Scots

Henry,
Bishop of
Winchester
(c.1099–1171)

Philippe,
Bishop of
Châlons

Matilda (Maud)
(d.1120)
(drowned off Barfleur,
Normandy)
= 1115
Richard,
2nd Earl of Chester
(1094–1120)
(drowned off Barfleur,
Normandy)

Agnes
=
Hugues III,
Seigneur du Puiset

Baldwin
(c.1126–35)

Eustace IV,
Count of Boulogne
(c.1130/31–53)
= 1140
Constance
(c.1128–76)
daughter of Louis VI,
King of France
(m. 2nd, 1154, Raymond V,
Count of Toulouse)

William II,
Count of Boulogne
(c.1134–59)
(killed at Siege of Toulouse)
= c.1149
Isabel
(c.1137–99)
daughter of William de Warenne,
3rd Earl of Warenne and Surrey
(m. 2nd, 1164, Hameline,
Earl of Warenne & Surrey, natural son
of Geoffrey V, Count of Anjou & Maine)

Matilda
(b. & d. c.1133–5)

Mary,
Countess of Boulogne
(c.1136–82)
= c.1160
Matthew I,
Count of Boulogne
(d.1173)
(m. annulled 1169; died from
a wound received at Siege of
Driencourt)

House of Plantagenet

King Henry II (r.1154–89) was the founder and first king of the House of Plantagenet. The name 'House of Plantagenet' derived from the sprig of broom (*planta genista*) that was habitually worn by Henry II's father, Geoffrey V, Count of Anjou and Maine (1113–51). It was not used until the fifteenth century, however, when it was adopted by Richard, Duke of York. Henry's own nickname, 'Curtmantle', came from the short cloak that he wore.

Henry became King in 1154, even though his mother, Matilda, did not die until 1167. Through his father, he was also heir to the region of Anjou in France, and through his marriage to Eleanor of Aquitaine (1122–1204), former wife of Louis VII of France (1120–80), he acquired the Duchy of Aquitaine. This French inheritance, towards which Henry II devoted most of his energies, meant that later English monarchs were often engaged in battles to retain their French lands, until Mary I finally lost Calais in 1558.

Henry II believed strongly in law and order, but he faced opposition in his attempts to subject the clergy to secular law, especially from Thomas Becket, Archbishop of Canterbury (c.1118–70), who was eventually murdered. Henry II's later years were much vexed by the rebellious disobedience of his sons, yet, ironically, his succession proved to be a straight-forward matter.

Henry II's two eldest sons both

predeceased him. He was therefore succeeded by his third son, Richard *Coeur de Lion*, or 'Lionheart', so named because of the heroic reputation he gained in the Third Crusade to recapture the Holy Land from the Muslims.

Richard I (r.1189–99) spent most of his reign abroad, and died of wounds suffered while besieging the castle of Châlus in Limousin. His wife, Berengaria of Navarre (c.1163–c.1230), bore him no children, and was the only queen of England never to visit the country.

Richard I's youngest brother, John Lackland (so called since he lacked territory in early life), succeeded him. Feckless and unprincipled, John (r.1199–1216) had been involved in conspiracies against his father and brother. However, in the latter part of Richard I's reign, they forged friendly relations and he succeeded at his brother's request. Squabbles with the Pope led to John's excommunication (revoked in 1213), and his autocratic rule resulted in him being forced to sign the Magna Carta at Runnymede in 1215 by his nobles. This charter effectively recognised the rights and privileges of the barons, Church and freemen. John was also responsible for the murder of his nephew, Arthur, Duke of Brittany (1187–1203), the rightful heir to the throne.

John was succeeded by his eldest son, Henry III (r.1216–72), who was only nine years old. Henry III was regarded as a feeble figure, too easily influenced by his mother, and – like his father – at odds with the barons. In 1258, his brother-in-law, Simon de Montfort, Earl of Leicester (c.1208–65), forced him to accept the Provisions of Oxford, a system of baronial committees that supervised the government of the realm. Henry was responsible for the redesign of Westminster Abbey by French architects in 1245, and lived well into old age, during which time his eldest son, Edward, who had proved himself a brave and able warrior, was groomed to take the throne.

Edward I (r.1272–1307) was an outstanding warrior king and a great constitutional jurist, and he helped to shape many of the political institutions of England as we know them today. He continued to assert his rule over Scotland and managed to conquer the Welsh, presenting his son, Edward, as the first English Prince of Wales in 1301. Edward I died near Carlisle in 1307, just as he was about to launch another attack on the Scots.

Edward's son and successor, Edward II (r.1307–27), was known for indolence and levity. His unpopularity grew as his favourite companion, Piers Gaveston (c.1284–1312), was given increasing importance. Edward II inherited none of his father's battle skills and was famously defeated by Robert the Bruce and the Scots at Bannockburn, in 1314. He was married to Isabella of France (1295–1358), who was estranged from him for much of their marriage. In 1326, accompanied by her lover, Roger de Mortimer (1287–1330), Isabella came over from France, with the plan of putting her son, also Edward, on the throne. Edward II was caught in Wales in 1327, deposed and imprisoned in Berkeley Castle. His captors hoped he would die of disease, but his constitution proved robust. Later that year, he was ruthlessly murdered with a red-hot poker, his dying shrieks resounding through the castle.

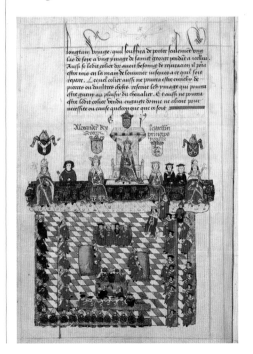

LEFT
Edward I in Parliament, from the sixteenth-century *Wriothesley Garter Book*. In this imagined view, the King is flanked by Alexander III of Scotland (1241–86) and Llywelyn the Last, Prince of Wales (c.1223–82), who probably did not attend the same Parliament. Also shown are justices, law officers, clerks, temporal lords, bishops and abbots.

House of Plantagenet

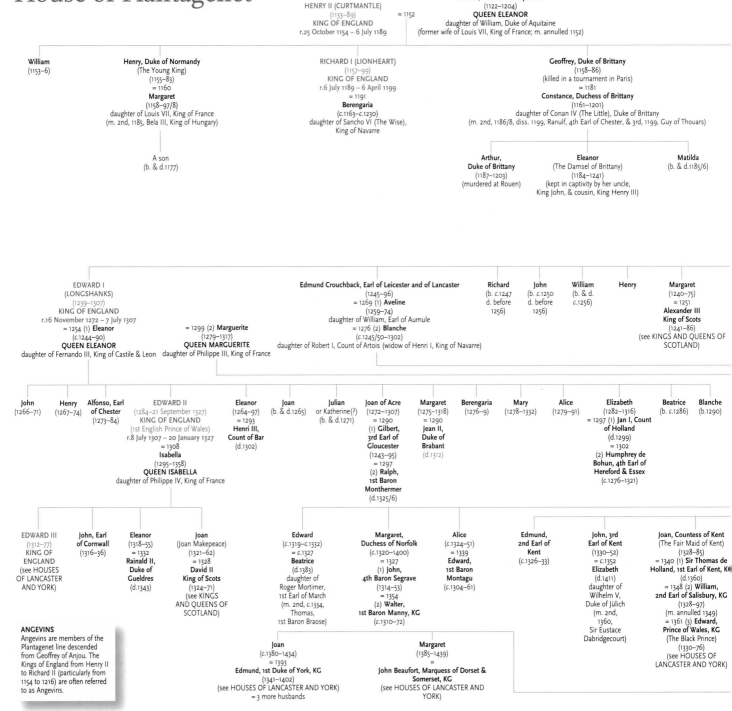

HENRY II (CURTMANTLE)
(1133–89)
KING OF ENGLAND
r.25 October 1154 – 6 July 1189
= 1152

Eleanor, Duchess of Aquitaine
(1122–1204)
QUEEN ELEANOR
daughter of William, Duke of Aquitaine
(former wife of Louis VII, King of France; m. annulled 1152)

William
(1153–6)

Henry, Duke of Normandy
(The Young King)
(1155–83)
= 1160
Margaret
(1158–97/8)
daughter of Louis VII, King of France
(m. 2nd, 1185, Bela III, King of Hungary)

A son
(b. & d.1177)

RICHARD I (LIONHEART)
(1157–99)
KING OF ENGLAND
r.6 July 1189 – 6 April 1199
= 1191
Berengaria
(c.1163–c.1230)
daughter of Sancho VI (The Wise),
King of Navarre

Geoffrey, Duke of Brittany
(1158–86)
(killed in a tournament in Paris)
= 1181
Constance, Duchess of Brittany
(1161–1201)
daughter of Conan IV (The Little), Duke of Brittany
(m. 2nd, 1186/8, diss. 1199, Ranulf, 4th Earl of Chester, & 3rd, 1199, Guy of Thouars)

Arthur, Duke of Brittany
(1187–1203)
(murdered at Rouen)

Eleanor
(The Damsel of Brittany)
(1184–1241)
(kept in captivity by her uncle,
King John, & cousin, King Henry III)

Matilda
(b. & d.1185/6)

EDWARD I (LONGSHANKS)
(1239–1307)
KING OF ENGLAND
r.16 November 1272 – 7 July 1307
= 1254 (1) **Eleanor**
(c.1244–90)
QUEEN ELEANOR
daughter of Fernando III, King of Castile & Leon

= 1299 (2) **Marguerite**
(1279–1317)
QUEEN MARGUERITE
daughter of Philippe III, King of France

Edmund Crouchback, Earl of Leicester and of Lancaster
(1245–96)
= 1269 (1) **Aveline**
(1259–74)
daughter of William, Earl of Aumule
= 1276 (2) **Blanche**
(c.1245/50–1302)
daughter of Robert I, Count of Artois (widow of Henri I, King of Navarre)

Richard
(b. c.1247
d. before
1256)

John
(b. c.1250
d. before
1256)

William
(b. & d.
c.1256)

Henry

Margaret
(1240–75)
= 1251
Alexander III
King of Scots
(1241–86)
(see KINGS AND QUEENS OF
SCOTLAND)

John
(1266–71)

Henry
(1267–74)

Alfonso, Earl of Chester
(1273–84)

EDWARD II
(1284–21 September 1327)
KING OF ENGLAND
(1st English Prince of Wales)
r.8 July 1307 – 20 January 1327
= 1308
Isabella
(1295–1358)
QUEEN ISABELLA
daughter of Philippe IV, King of France

Eleanor
(1264–97)
= 1293
**Henri III,
Count of Bar**
(d.1302)

Joan
(b. & d.1265)

**Julian
or Katherine(?)**
(b. & d.1271)

Joan of Acre
(1272–1307)
= 1290
(1) **Gilbert,
3rd Earl of
Gloucester**
(1243–95)
= 1297
(2) **Ralph,
1st Baron
Monthermer**
(d.1325/6)

Margaret
(1275–1318)
= 1290
**Jean II,
Duke of
Brabant**
(d.1312)

Berengaria
(1276–9)

Mary
(1278–1332)

Alice
(1279–91)

Elizabeth
(1282–1316)
= 1297 (1) **Jan I, Count
of Holland**
(d.1299)
= 1302
(2) **Humphrey de
Bohun, 4th Earl of
Hereford & Essex**
(c.1276–1321)

Beatrice
(b. c.1286)

Blanche
(b.1290)

EDWARD III
(1312–77)
KING OF
ENGLAND
(see HOUSES
OF LANCASTER
AND YORK)

**John, Earl
of Cornwall**
(1316–36)

Eleanor
(1318–55)
= 1332
**Rainald II,
Duke of
Gueldres**
(d.1343)

Joan
(Joan Makepeace)
(1321–62)
= 1328
**David II
King of Scots**
(1324–71)
(see KINGS
AND QUEENS OF
SCOTLAND)

ANGEVINS
Angevins are members of the
Plantagenet line descended
from Geoffrey of Anjou. The
Kings of England from Henry II
to Richard II (particularly from
1154 to 1216) are often referred
to as Angevins.

Edward
(c.1300–c.1332)
= c.1327
Beatrice
(d.1383)
daughter of
Roger Mortimer,
1st Earl of March
(m. 2nd, c.1334,
Thomas,
1st Baron Braose)

**Margaret,
Duchess of Norfolk**
(c.1320–1400)
= 1327
(1) **John,
4th Baron Segrave**
(1314–53)
= 1354
(2) **Walter,
1st Baron Manny, KG**
(c.1310–72)

Alice
(c.1324–51)
= 1339
**Edward,
1st Baron
Montagu**
(c.1304–61)

**Edmund,
2nd Earl of
Kent**
(c.1326–33)

**John, 3rd
Earl of Kent**
(1330–52)
= c.1352
Elizabeth
(d.1411)
daughter of
Wilhelm V,
Duke of Jülich
(m. 2nd,
1360,
Sir Eustace
Dabridgecourt)

Joan, Countess of Kent
(The Fair Maid of Kent)
(1328–85)
= 1340 (1) **Sir Thomas de
Holland, 1st Earl of Kent, KG**
(d.1360)
= 1348 (2) **William,
2nd Earl of Salisbury, KG**
(1328–97)
(m. annulled 1349)
= 1361 (3) **Edward,
Prince of Wales, KG**
(The Black Prince)
(1330–76)
(see HOUSES OF
LANCASTER AND YORK)

Joan
(c.1380–1434)
= 1393
Edmund, 1st Duke of York, KG
(1341–1402)
(see HOUSES OF LANCASTER AND YORK)
= 3 more husbands

Margaret
(1385–1439)
=
**John Beaufort, Marquess of Dorset &
Somerset, KG**
(see HOUSES OF LANCASTER AND
YORK)

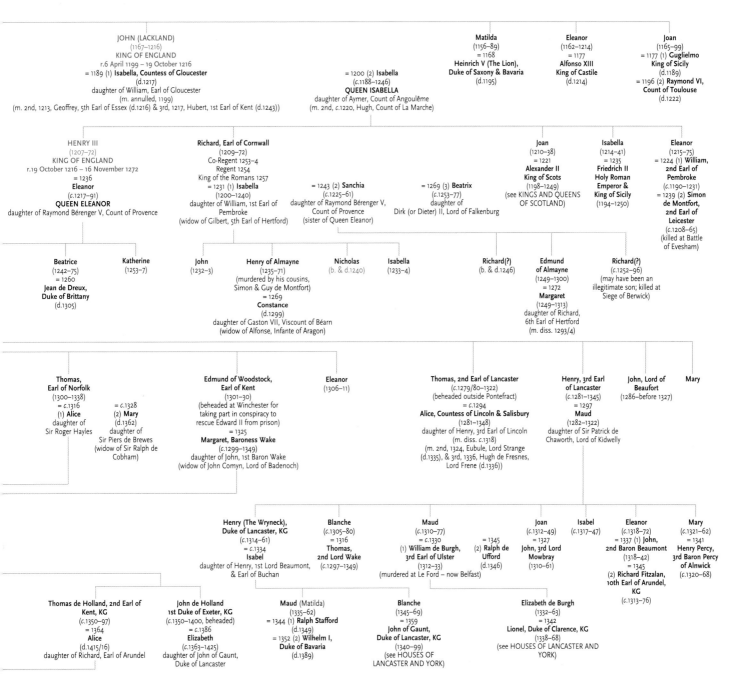

JOHN (LACKLAND)
(1167–1216)
KING OF ENGLAND
r.6 April 1199 – 19 October 1216
= 1189 (1) Isabella, Countess of Gloucester
(d.1217)
daughter of William, Earl of Gloucester
(m. annulled, 1199)
(m. 2nd, 1213, Geoffrey, 5th Earl of Essex (d.1216) & 3rd, 1217, Hubert, 1st Earl of Kent (d.1243))

= 1200 (2) Isabella
(c.1188–1246)
QUEEN ISABELLA
daughter of Aymer, Count of Angoulême
(m. 2nd, c.1220, Hugh, Count of La Marche)

Matilda
(1156–89)
= 1168
Heinrich V (The Lion),
Duke of Saxony & Bavaria
(d.1195)

Eleanor
(1162–1214)
= 1177
Alfonso XIII
King of Castile
(d.1214)

Joan
(1165–99)
= 1177 (1) Guglielmo
King of Sicily
(d.1189)
= 1196 (2) Raymond VI,
Count of Toulouse
(d.1222)

HENRY III
(1207–72)
KING OF ENGLAND
r.19 October 1216 – 16 November 1272
= 1236
Eleanor
(c.1217–91)
QUEEN ELEANOR
daughter of Raymond Bérenger V, Count of Provence

Richard, Earl of Cornwall
(1209–72)
Co-Regent 1253–4
Regent 1254
King of the Romans 1257
= 1231 (1) Isabella
(1200–1240)
daughter of William, 1st Earl of
Pembroke
(widow of Gilbert, 5th Earl of Hertford)

= 1243 (2) Sanchia
(c.1225–61)
daughter of Raymond Bérenger V,
Count of Provence
(sister of Queen Eleanor)

= 1269 (3) Beatrix
(c.1253–77)
daughter of
Dirk (or Dieter) II, Lord of Falkenburg

Joan
(1210–38)
= 1221
Alexander II
King of Scots
(1198–1249)
(see KINGS AND QUEENS
OF SCOTLAND)

Isabella
(1214–41)
= 1235
Friedrich II
Holy Roman
Emperor &
King of Sicily
(1194–1250)

Eleanor
(1215–75)
= 1224 (1) William,
2nd Earl of
Pembroke
(c.1190–1231)
= 1239 (2) Simon
de Montfort,
2nd Earl of
Leicester
(c.1208–65)
(killed at Battle
of Evesham)

Beatrice
(1242–75)
= 1260
Jean de Dreux,
Duke of Brittany
(d.1305)

Katherine
(1253–7)

John
(1232–3)

Henry of Almayne
(1235–71)
(murdered by his cousins,
Simon & Guy de Montfort)
= 1269
Constance
(d.1299)
daughter of Gaston VII, Viscount of Béarn
(widow of Alfonse, Infante of Aragon)

Nicholas
(b. & d.1240)

Isabella
(1233–4)

Richard(?)
(b. & d.1246)

Edmund
of Almayne
(1249–1300)
= 1272
Margaret
(1249–1313)
daughter of Richard,
6th Earl of Hertford
(m. diss. 1293/4)

Richard(?)
(c.1252–96)
(may have been an
illegitimate son; killed at
Siege of Berwick)

Thomas,
Earl of Norfolk
(1300–1338)
= c.1316
(1) Alice
daughter of
Sir Roger Hayles

= c.1328
(2) Mary
(d.1362)
daughter of
Sir Piers de Brewes
(widow of Sir Ralph de
Cobham)

Edmund of Woodstock,
Earl of Kent
(1301–30)
(beheaded at Winchester for
taking part in conspiracy to
rescue Edward II from prison)
= 1325
Margaret, Baroness Wake
(c.1299–1349)
daughter of John, 1st Baron Wake
(widow of John Comyn, Lord of Badenoch)

Eleanor
(1306–11)

Thomas, 2nd Earl of Lancaster
(c.1279/80–1322)
(beheaded outside Pontefract)
= c.1294
Alice, Countess of Lincoln & Salisbury
(1281–1348)
daughter of Henry, 3rd Earl of Lincoln
(m. diss. c.1318)
(m. 2nd, 1324, Eubule, Lord Strange
(d.1335), & 3rd, 1336, Hugh de Fresnes,
Lord Frene (d.1336))

Henry, 3rd Earl
of Lancaster
(c.1281–1345)
= 1297
Maud
(1282–1322)
daughter of Sir Patrick de
Chaworth, Lord of Kidwelly

John, Lord of
Beaufort
(1286–before 1327)

Mary

Henry (The Wryneck),
Duke of Lancaster, KG
(c.1314–61)
= c.1334
Isabel
daughter of Henry, 1st Lord Beaumont,
& Earl of Buchan

Blanche
(c.1305–80)
= 1316
Thomas,
2nd Lord Wake
(c.1297–1349)

Maud
(c.1310–77)
= c.1330
(1) William de Burgh,
3rd Earl of Ulster
(1312–33)
(murdered at Le Ford – now Belfast)

= 1345
(2) Ralph de
Ufford
(d.1346)

Joan
(c.1312–49)
= 1327
John, 3rd Lord
Mowbray
(1310–61)

Isabel
(c.1317–47)

Eleanor
(c.1318–72)
= 1337 (1) John,
2nd Baron Beaumont
(1318–42)
= 1345
(2) Richard Fitzalan,
10th Earl of Arundel,
KG
(c.1313–76)

Mary
(c.1321–62)
= 1341
Henry Percy,
3rd Baron Percy
of Alnwick
(c.1320–68)

Thomas de Holland, 2nd Earl of
Kent, KG
(c.1350–97)
= 1364
Alice
(d.1415/16)
daughter of Richard, Earl of Arundel

John de Holland
1st Duke of Exeter, KG
(c.1350–1400, beheaded)
= c.1386
Elizabeth
(c.1363–1425)
daughter of John of Gaunt,
Duke of Lancaster

Maud (Matilda)
(1335–62)
= 1344 (1) Ralph Stafford
(d.1349)
= 1352 (2) Wilhelm I,
Duke of Bavaria
(d.1389)

Blanche
(1345–69)
= 1359
John of Gaunt,
Duke of Lancaster, KG
(1340–99)
(see HOUSES OF
LANCASTER AND YORK)

Elizabeth de Burgh
(1332–63)
= 1342
Lionel, Duke of Clarence, KG
(1338–68)
(see HOUSES OF LANCASTER AND
YORK)

Houses of Lancaster and York

The line of descent from Edward III to Henry VII runs through more than 150 years of some of the most dramatic events and conflicts in the history of England.

Edward III (r.1327–77) was placed on the throne by his mother, Queen Isabella, and her lover, Roger de Mortimer. The King married Philippa of Hainault (c.1312–69) at their instigation, and it proved to be a happy marriage. Edward III laid claim to the kingdom of France through his mother, and, aided by his son, Edward, won victories at the battle of Crécy (1346) and the conquest of Calais (1347). These conflicts were the start of the Hundred Years War between England and France. In 1348, Edward founded the Order of the Garter, the senior order of British chivalry.

Edward III had seven sons, five of whom played a significant part in history: Edward, the Black Prince (1330–76); Lionel, Duke of Clarence (1338–68) (the Yorkist party based their claim to the throne on descent from Philippa, his daughter by his first marriage); John of Gaunt,

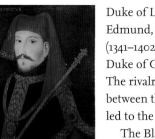

Duke of Lancaster (1340–99); Edmund, Duke of York (1341–1402); and Thomas, Duke of Gloucester (1355–97). The rivalry that sprang up between their descendants led to the Wars of the Roses.

The Black Prince died in 1376, so on the death of Edward III the following year, the throne passed to the Black Prince's surviving son, Richard II (r.1377–99). In 1381, when he was only 14, Richard bravely quelled the Peasants' Revolt, led by Wat Tyler (1341–81). Richard's uncles were constantly jostling for power, and for a long time, Thomas, Duke of Gloucester, held considerable sway at court. Later, with the help of another uncle, John of Gaunt, Richard overthrew Gloucester and his supporters. Richard II reigned until he was coerced into giving up the throne in September 1399, by his first cousin, Henry, Duke of Lancaster, son of John of Gaunt (who had died in February that year). Richard died, childless, in prison at Pontefract Castle, in February 1400.

Parliament consented to Henry, Duke of Lancaster, becoming King, and, as Henry IV (r.1399–1413), he was the first King of the House of Lancaster. His son, Henry V (r.1413–22), is best remembered for his great victory against the French at Agincourt in 1415, and for realising the importance to

ROYAL TITLES

In the peerage of England, the heir apparent is automatically Duke of Cornwall if he is the eldest son of the sovereign, and in Scotland he is Duke of Rothesay, Earl of Carrick, Baron of Renfrew, Lord of the Isles and Great Steward of Scotland. Richard, second son of King John, was also Earl of Cornwall, but the title died out in 1300. Cornwall has been associated with the heir to the throne since Edward III created his son, Edward, Duke of Cornwall in 1337. The Scottish titles date back to 1398.

The title of Earl of Chester was conferred on Edward, eldest son of Henry III, in 1254. In 1301, Edward I conferred the title of Prince of Wales on his eldest surviving son, who became Edward II in 1307. Edward II gave his son (later Edward III) the earldom of Chester. Since the days of Edward III, the two titles have always been conferred together. In 1911, Edward, son of George V, was formally invested as Prince of Wales at Caernarvon Castle, as was Prince Charles in 1969.

The title of Duke of York, which has come to be bestowed on the second son of the sovereign, has always been a royal title. It was first conferred on Edmund, fifth son of Edward III, by Richard II, in 1385. The title has frequently reverted to the Crown, as several dukes of York have become Prince of Wales or king. The title is currently held by Prince Andrew.

The title of Duke of Gloucester has always been a royal one. The first duke was Thomas of Woodstock, seventh son of Edward III. Perhaps the most famous holder of the title was the future Richard III. The title has sometimes died out, but has been revived periodically: in 1659, for the youngest son of Charles I; in 1689, for Queen Anne's sole surviving child; in 1764, for a brother of George III; and in 1928, for Prince Henry, third son of King George V. It is now held by Prince Henry's second and only surviving son, Prince Richard.

Britain of sea power. He was duly succeeded by his son, Henry VI (r.1422–61, 1470–71), during whose reign the French expelled the English from most of northern France. Henry VI was considered weak, and was plagued by intermittent periods of insanity. During these periods, Richard, 3rd Duke of York (1411–60), served as Protector (1454–5 and 1455–6). Open rivalries between the Duke of York and Edmund, 1st Duke of Somerset (1406–55), erupted into the bloody conflict known as the Wars of the Roses (1455–85), named after the heraldic badges of the Houses of York and Lancaster.

During the course of these wars, Richard, Duke of York, captured Henry VI at Northampton, in 1460, and forced Henry to acknowledge him as Protector and Defender of the Realm. In the same year, Richard was killed in battle, and in 1461, his son deposed Henry VI and succeeded as Edward IV (r.1461–70, 1471–83).

Henry VI took refuge in Scotland, but was captured and imprisoned in the Tower of London in 1464. He was placed on the throne again briefly in 1470, by Richard Neville, 'the Kingmaker', 1st Earl of Warwick (1428–71). But Edward IV crushed the Lancastrians at the battles of Barnet and Tewkesbury in 1471, killed Edward, Prince of Wales (1453–71), and had Henry secretly murdered. Recovering the throne, and retaining it until his death, Edward IV became the first Sovereign of the House of York. He was also the first King to address Parliament in person. He allowed many great nobles to build large power bases in the provinces, in return for their support.

In 1483, the crown passed to Edward V (r.April–June 1483), the eldest son of Edward IV, who was then a boy of 12. His guardian was his uncle, Richard, Duke of

LEFT
The official 60th birthday photograph of HRH The Prince of Wales, taken by Hugo Burnand at Clarence House in February 2008. It shows His Royal Highness in the ceremonial uniform of the Welsh Guards.

BELOW
British School, *Henry VI*, sixteenth century.

surviving branch of the House of Lancaster. It was a weak claim, as Henry's mother was a descendant of John of Gaunt's third marriage, the children of which had been born out of wedlock. They were legitimised by royal charter in 1397, but were barred from succession to the throne.

Henry defeated Richard III's armies in 1485, at the battle of Bosworth (where Richard was killed), and mounted the throne as Henry VII, his title being confirmed by an Act of Parliament. Wisely, he married Elizabeth, eldest daughter of Edward IV and heiress of the House of York, thus uniting the rival claims of Edward III's descendants to form the new Tudor dynasty.

Gloucester (who, it was said, had already been responsible for drowning his own brother, George, Duke of Clarence (1449–78), in a butt of Malmsey wine, for siding with the Earl of Warwick). Later that year, Edward V was imprisoned in the Tower with his brother, Richard, Duke of York (1473–c.1483), and they were never seen in public again. Although Richard III has been blamed for their murders, there is also a lasting theory that they survived his reign and that it was the future Henry VII who had them killed.

The Duke of Gloucester succeeded to the throne as Richard III (r.1483–5). The death of his ten-year-old son in 1484 prompted him to nominate his nephew, John, Earl of Lincoln (d.1487), as heir. However, the Lancastrians put forward their own champion, Henry Tudor, Earl of Richmond, whose mother, Margaret Beaufort (1443–1509), was descended from the only

Houses of Lancaster and York

EDWARD III
(1312–77)
KING OF ENGLAND
r.20 January 1327 – 21 June 1377
= 1328

Philippa
(c.1312–69)
QUEEN PHILIPPA
daughter of Guillaume I, Count of Hainault

Edward, the Black Prince, Prince of Wales, KG
(1330–76)
= 1361
Joan, Countess of Kent
(1328–85)
(see HOUSE OF PLANTAGENET)

William
(b. & d.1337)

Lionel, Duke of Clarence, KG
(1338–68)
= 1342 (1) **Elizabeth de Burgh**
(1332–63)
daughter of William, 3rd Earl of Ulster,
and Maud, daughter of
3rd Earl of Lancaster
(see HOUSE OF PLANTAGENET)
= 1368 (2) **Violante**
(c.1353–86)
daughter of Galeazzo II (Visconti),
Lord of Milan

**John of Gaunt,
Duke of Lancaster, KG**
(1340–99)
= 1359 (1) **Blanche**
(1345–69)
daughter of Henry,
Duke of Lancaster, KG

= 1371 (2) **Constance, titular Queen of Castile
& Leon**
(1354–94)
daughter of Pedro I (The Cruel), King of Castile
& Leon

= 1396 (3) **Catherine**
(1350–1403)
daughter of Sir Payn Roet
(widow of Sir Hugh Swynford)

Edward of Angoulême
(1365–72)

RICHARD II
(1367–1400)
KING OF ENGLAND
r.21 June 1377 – 29 September 1399
= 1382 (1) **Anne**
(1366–94)
QUEEN ANNE
daughter of Karl IV, Holy Roman Emperor
= 1396 (2) **Isabelle**
(1389–1409)
QUEEN ISABELLE
daughter of Charles VI of France
(m. 2nd, 1406, Charles,
Duke of Orleans (d.1465))

John of Gaunt
(b.1374)

Catherine
(1372/3–1418)
= 1393
Enrique III, KG
King of Castile
& Leon
(d.1406)

**John Beaufort,
Marquess of Dorset
& Somerset, KG**
(c.1373–1410)
= 1397
Margaret
(1385–1439)
daughter of Thomas de Holland,
2nd Earl of Kent, KG
(see HOUSE OF PLANTAGENET)
(m. 2nd, 1412, Thomas, Duke of
Clarence, KG, 2nd son
of King Henry IV)

**Henry Beaufort,
Bishop of
Winchester &
Chancellor of
England**
(c.1375–1447)

John
(b. c.1362)

Edward
(b. c.1365)

John
(b. c.1366)

HENRY IV
Duke of Lancaster
(1367–1413)
KING OF ENGLAND
r.29 September 1399 – 20 March 1413
= 1380 (1) **Mary**
(c.1370–94)
daughter of
Humphrey de Bohun,
7th Earl of Hereford &
2nd Earl of Northampton, KG
= 1403 (2) **Joan,
Duchess of Brittany**
(c.1370–1437)
QUEEN JOAN
daughter of Charles II,
King of Navarre

Philippa
(1360–1415)
= 1387
João I, KG
King of Portugal
(d.1433)

Elizabeth
(c.1363–1425)
= 1380 (1) **John Hastings,
Earl of Pembroke**
(m. diss. c.1383)
= c.1386 (2) **John de Holland,
1st Duke of Exeter, KG**
(half-brother of King Richard II;
beheaded 1400)
= 1400 (3) **John Cornwall, 1st Baron
Fanhope of Fanhope, KG**
(d.1443)

Isabel
(b. c.1368)

**Henry,
2nd Earl
of Somerset**
(1401–18)

**John, 3rd Earl
of Somerset, KG**
(1404–44)
= 1439
Margaret
daughter of John,
3rd Baron Beauchamp of Bletso
(widow of Sir Oliver St John;
m. 3rd, Leo, 6th Baron Wells, KG)

**Thomas, Earl
of Perche**
(1405–32)

A son
(b.1382)

HENRY V
(1387–1422)
KING OF ENGLAND
r.20 March 1413 – 31 August 1422
= 1420
Catherine
(1401–37)
QUEEN CATHERINE
daughter of Charles VI, King of France
(m. 2nd(?), c.1428, Owen Tudor)

**Thomas, Duke of
Clarence, KG**
(1388–1421)
(killed at Battle
of Bougé)
= 1412
**Margaret, Countess
of Somerset**
(1385–1439)
daughter of Thomas
de Holland,
2nd Earl of Kent, KG

**John, Duke of
Bedford, KG**
(1389–1435)
= 1423 (1) **Anne**
(1404/5–32)
daughter of John,
Duke of Burgundy
= 1433 (2) **Jacquette**
(c.1416–72)
daughter of Pierre de
Luxembourg,
Count of St Pol
(m. 2nd, c.1436,
Richard Woodville,
1st Earl Rivers, KG)

**Humphrey, Duke of
Gloucester, KG**
(1390–1447)
Regent of England 1420–21,
Protector 1422 & 1427–9,
Lieutenant of the Kingdom
1430–32
= 1422 (1) **Jacqueline**
(d.1436)
daughter of Willem VI,
Count of Holland
(former wife of Jean IV,
Duke of Brabant, & widow
of Jean of France,
Dauphin of Viennois)
(m. annulled 1428)
= (2) **Eleanor**
(d. c.1454)
daughter of Reginald,
2nd Baron Cobham of
Sterborough

Blanche
(1392–1409)
= 1402
Ludwig III,
Duke of
Bavaria,
Elector
Palatine
of the Rhine
(d.1436)

Philippa
(1394–1430)
= 1406
Eric IX, KG
King of
Denmark,
Sweden &
Norway

**Margaret
Beaufort**
(1443–1509)
= 1455 (1) **Edmund
Tudor, 1st Earl
of Richmond**
(c.1430–56)
son of Owen Tudor
& Catherine, widow
of King Henry V
= (2) **Lord Henry
Stafford**
(d.1471)
= (3) **Thomas
Stanley,
1st Earl of
Derby, KG**
(d.1504)

= c.1459

**Henry Beaufort,
2nd Duke of
Somerset**
(1436–64)
(beheaded after a fight
at Hexham, against
the Yorkists)

from his son,
**Charles Somerset,
Earl of Worcester**
(b. c.1460)
descend the dukes of
Beaufort, of whom the
10th Duke (1900–1984)
married Lady Mary Cambridge
(1897–1987)
daughter of Adolphus,
1st Marquess of Cambridge
(see FAMILY OF
GEORGE III)

HENRY VI
(1421–21 May 1471)
KING OF ENGLAND
r.31 August 1422 – 4 March 1461,
3 October 1470 – 11 April 1471
= 1445
Margaret
(1429–82)
QUEEN MARGARET
daughter of René, Duke of Anjou,
titular King of Naples & Sicily

HENRY VII
(1457–1509)
KING OF ENGLAND
(see HOUSE OF TUDOR)

Edward, Prince of Wales
(1453–71)
= 1470
Anne
(1456–85)
daughter of Richard, 1st Earl of Warwick
& 2nd Earl of Salisbury, KG
(m. 2nd, 1472, Richard, Duke of
Gloucester, later King Richard III)

EDWARD V
(1470–c.1483)
KING OF ENGLAND
r.9 April – 25 June 1483
(presumed murdered in the
Tower of London)

**Richard, Duke
of York, KG**
(1473–c.1483)
(presumed murdered in
the Tower of London)
= 1478
Anne
(1472–81)
daughter of John Mowbray,
4th Duke of Norfolk, KG

**George, Duke
of Bedford**
(1477–9)

Elizabeth
(1466–1503)
= 1486
HENRY VII
(1457–1509)
KING OF ENGLAND
(see HOUSE OF
TUDOR)

Mary
(1467–82)

Cicely
(1469–1507)
= 1487
(1) **John, 1st
Viscount
Welles, KG**
(d.1499)
= 1504
(2) **Thomas Kyrme**

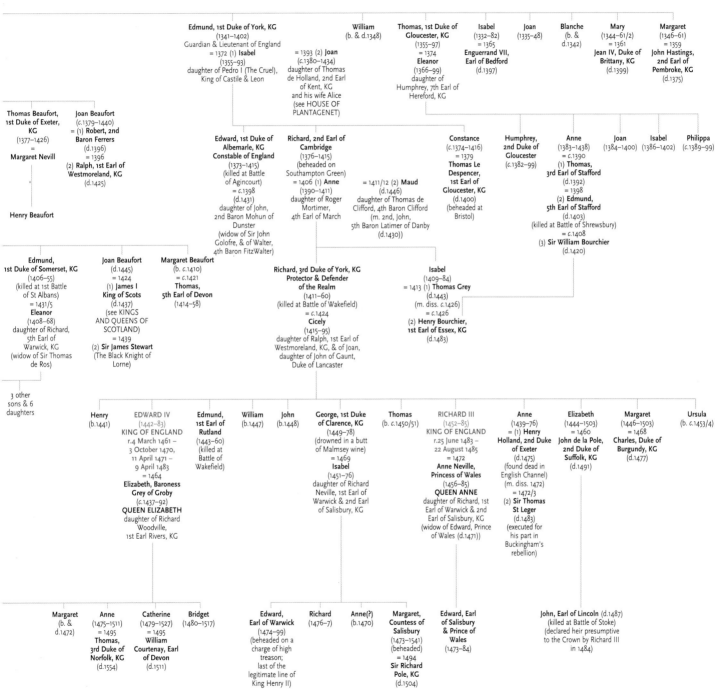

House of Tudor

RIGHT
Unknown artist, *Henry VII*, sixteenth century.

BELOW
After Hans Holbein the Younger, *Henry VIII*, sixteenth century.

The House of Tudor lasted for nearly 120 years, but comprised only three generations (or four, including Lady Jane Grey). Henry VII's wife, Elizabeth of York (1466–1503), was the daughter of Edward IV, sister of Edward V and, by 1485, heir to the House of York. Thus the 'red rose' of Lancaster finally united with the 'white rose' of York, giving their descendants an inalienable right to sit on the throne of England. Henry descended from the kings of France and the native princes of Wales through his father, Edmund Tudor (c.1430–56).

Henry VII's paternal grandmother was Catherine of France (1401–37), daughter of King Charles VI (1368–1422). His mother, Lady Margaret Beaufort, was alive when he took the throne, and in fact outlived her son by three months.

Henry VII (r.1485–1509) enjoyed a successful reign and concentrated on maintaining stability in the country after years of warfare. He undertook many building projects and founded religious houses. His son and heir, Arthur, Prince of Wales (1486–1502), married Catherine of Aragon (1485–1536), but died at the age of 15. Arthur was succeeded by his brother, Henry VIII (r.1509–47).

Henry VIII's life was dominated by the need to produce a male heir. He married his brother's widow in 1509. Catherine produced six children, but only one child – a daughter – survived, subsequently becoming Mary I. Henry broke from Rome after the Pope refused to annul his marriage; he divorced Catherine in order to marry Anne Boleyn (c.1501/2–36), who bore him the future Elizabeth I. Anne Boleyn was executed on a charge of adultery, and Henry married Jane Seymour (c.1505–37), mother of Edward VI. Jane died shortly after giving birth, and there were three subsequent Queens: Anne of Cleves (1515–57), whose marriage was annulled; Catherine Howard (1521/2–42), who was executed; and Catherine Parr (1512–48), who survived the King.

An extravagant figure, with a Renaissance education, Henry looms large over history. By the Acts of Annates, Appeals and

BELOW
Unknown artist, *The Family of Henry VIII*, c.1545.

Supremacy, he declared himself Supreme Head of the Church, and, by no longer paying funds into the papal treasury, he repudiated the Pope's ecclesiastical authority in England. These radical changes to the Church continued with the Dissolution of the Monasteries in 1536 and 1539. Henry also united Wales with England by the Statutes of Wales of 1534–6.

Henry VIII was succeeded by his only son, Edward VI (r.1547–53), then aged only nine. Edward's short reign was overshadowed by the protectorate of his maternal uncle, Edward Seymour, Duke of Somerset (c.1506–52), to whose execution Edward assented, and then by that of John Dudley, Earl of Warwick (1504–53), created Duke of Northumberland in 1551.

Edward VI named as his successor Lady Jane Grey (1537–54), who was the granddaughter of Henry VII's third daughter, Mary (1496–1533). Henry VIII had left the crown to Mary's descendants, rather than those of his elder sister, Margaret, Queen of Scotland (1489–1541), should his own issue fail. Lady Jane Grey's accession threatened the senior lineal heirs, Mary and Elizabeth, and the royal House of Scotland, which descended from Margaret.

The Duke of Northumberland arranged Lady Jane's marriage to his son, Guilford Dudley (d.1554), and set up his reluctant daughter-in-law on the throne, on the grounds that Mary and Elizabeth had both been declared illegitimate. However, the country rallied behind Mary Tudor, the rightful Queen. Jane was overthrown and executed, with her husband, at the Tower of London, in February 1554, after a reign of just nine days.

Mary I (r.1553–8) had been in line to the throne, but after her mother's death, in 1536, she was forced to sign a declaration acknowledging that her parents' union had been illegal and that she was illegitimate. After Edward VI died, Mary's claim to the throne was recognised and she was crowned in 1553.

Mary, a devout Catholic, was much influenced by her cousin, Emperor Charles V (1500–58), and she married his son, Philip II of Spain (1527–98), thereby alienating the English people. Her determination to restore papal supremacy led to a rebellion (quelled in 1554), and a phase of religious persecutions that earned her the nickname 'Bloody Mary'. Deserted by Philip in 1557, she died, childless, a year later.

Mary I's half-sister and successor was the last of the Tudors. Like Mary, Elizabeth had been declared illegitimate when her mother fell from grace, but her reign as Elizabeth I, the Virgin Queen (r.1558–1603), is remembered as a glorious one, notable for the victory of the English fleet over the Spanish Armada in 1588 and the flowering of the English Renaissance.

Elizabeth never married, and on her death the succession was again in doubt. In the end, despite the threat that had been posed by Mary, Queen of Scots (1542–87), to the English throne (Elizabeth had her cousin executed in 1587), it was to Mary's son, James VI of Scotland, that Elizabeth entrusted her kingdom.

House of Tudor

HENRY VII
(1457–1509)
KING OF ENGLAND
r.22 August 1485 – 21 April 1509

= 1486

Princess Elizabeth of York
(1466–1503)
QUEEN ELIZABETH
daughter of King Edward IV
(see HOUSES OF
LANCASTER AND YORK)

**Arthur, Prince
of Wales, KG**
(1486–1502)
= 1501
Catherine of Aragon
(1485–1536)
daughter of Ferdinand V,
King of Aragon,
and Isabelle I,
Queen of Castile & Leon

HENRY VIII
(1491–1547)
KING OF ENGLAND
r.21 April 1509 –
28 January 1547

= 1509 (1) **Catherine of
Aragon,
Princess of Wales**
(1485–1536)
QUEEN CATHERINE
(m. declared null 1533,
diss. 1534)

= 1533 (2) **Anne Boleyn,
Marchioness of Pembroke**
(c.1501/2–36)
QUEEN ANNE
daughter of Thomas Boleyn, 1st
Earl of Wiltshire & Ormonde, KG
(m. declared invalid 1536;
beheaded)

= 1536
(3) **Jane Seymour**
(c.1505–37)
QUEEN JANE
daughter of
Sir John Seymour

= 1540
(4) **Anne of Cleves**
(1515–57)
QUEEN ANNE
daughter of Johann III,
Duke of Cleves
(m. annulled 1540)

= 1540
(5) **Catherine Howard**
(1521/2–42)
QUEEN CATHERINE
daughter of Lord Edmund
Howard (son of Thomas Howard,
2nd Duke of Norfolk, KG)
(beheaded)

= 1543
(6) **Catherine Parr**
(1512–48)
QUEEN CATHERINE
daughter of Sir Thomas Parr
(widow of John Nevill,
3rd Baron Latimer, & of
Sir Edward Borough)

**Henry, Duke of
Cornwall**
(b. & d.1511)

**A son (Henry?),
Duke of Cornwall**
(b. & d.1513)

A son
(1514)
(stillborn?)

A daughter
(1510)
(stillborn)

MARY I
(1516–58)
QUEEN OF ENGLAND
r.19 July 1553 –
17 November 1558
= 1554
Philip II
King of Spain, KG
(1527–98)

A daughter
(1518)
(stillborn)

A son
(1534)
(stillborn)

A son
(1536)
(stillborn)

ELIZABETH I
(1533–1603)
QUEEN OF ENGLAND
r.17 November 1558 –
24 March 1603

EDWARD VI
(1537–53)
KING OF ENGLAND
r.28 January 1547 –
6 July 1553

Attributed to the British
School, *Catherine of
Aragon*, sixteenth/
seventeenth century.

Attributed to the British
School, *Anne Boleyn*,
sixteenth/seventeenth
century.

Hans Holbein the
Younger, *Jane Seymour*,
1536–7. Chalks, pen and
ink, and metalpoint on
paper.

Hans Holbein the
Younger, *Anne of Cleves*,
1539. Watercolour on
vellum.

Hans Holbein the
Younger, *Portrait of a
lady, perhaps Katherine
Howard*, c.1540.
Watercolour on vellum.

William Scrots
(fl. 1537–53),
Catherine Parr.

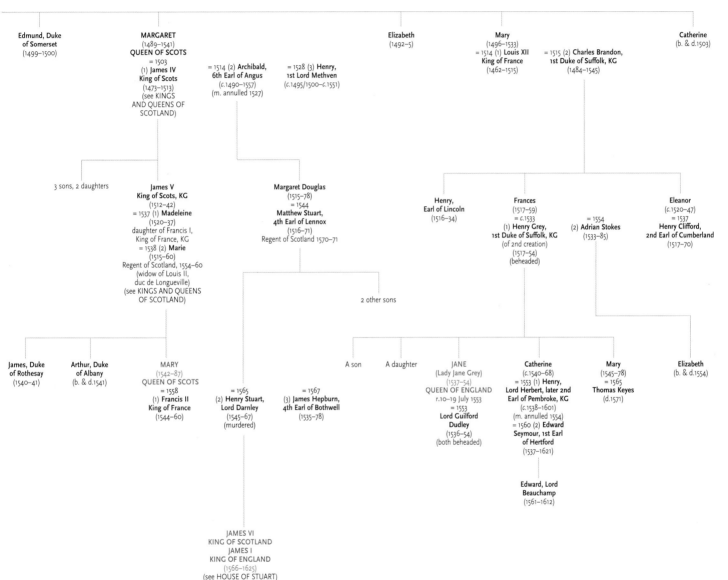

Edmund, Duke
of Somerset
(1499–1500)

MARGARET
(1489–1541)
QUEEN OF SCOTS
= 1503
(1) James IV
King of Scots
(1473–1513)
(see KINGS
AND QUEENS OF
SCOTLAND)

= 1514 (2) Archibald,
6th Earl of Angus
(c.1490–1557)
(m. annulled 1527)

= 1528 (3) Henry,
1st Lord Methven
(c.1495/1500–c.1551)

Elizabeth
(1492–5)

Mary
(1496–1533)
= 1514 (1) Louis XII
King of France
(1462–1515)

= 1515 (2) Charles Brandon,
1st Duke of Suffolk, KG
(1484–1545)

Catherine
(b. & d.1503)

3 sons, 2 daughters

James V
King of Scots, KG
(1512–42)
= 1537 (1) Madeleine
(1520–37)
daughter of Francis I,
King of France, KG
= 1538 (2) Marie
(1515–60)
Regent of Scotland, 1554–60
(widow of Louis II,
duc de Longueville)
(see KINGS AND QUEENS
OF SCOTLAND)

Margaret Douglas
(1515–78)
= 1544
Matthew Stuart,
4th Earl of Lennox
(1516–71)
Regent of Scotland 1570–71

Henry,
Earl of Lincoln
(1516–34)

Frances
(1517–59)
= c.1533
(1) Henry Grey,
1st Duke of Suffolk, KG
(of 2nd creation)
(1517–54)
(beheaded)

= 1554
(2) Adrian Stokes
(1533–85)

Eleanor
(c.1520–47)
= 1537
Henry Clifford,
2nd Earl of Cumberland
(1517–70)

James, Duke
of Rothesay
(1540–41)

Arthur, Duke
of Albany
(b. & d.1541)

MARY
(1542–87)
QUEEN OF SCOTS
= 1558
(1) Francis II
King of France
(1544–60)

= 1565
(2) Henry Stuart,
Lord Darnley
(1545–67)
(murdered)

= 1567
(3) James Hepburn,
4th Earl of Bothwell
(1535–78)

2 other sons

A son

A daughter

JANE
(Lady Jane Grey)
(1537–54)
QUEEN OF ENGLAND
r.10–19 July 1553
= 1553
Lord Guilford
Dudley
(1536–54)
(both beheaded)

Catherine
(c.1540–68)
= 1553 (1) Henry,
Lord Herbert, later 2nd
Earl of Pembroke, KG
(c.1538–1601)
(m. annulled 1554)
= 1560 (2) Edward
Seymour, 1st Earl
of Hertford
(1537–1621)

Mary
(1545–78)
= 1565
Thomas Keyes
(d.1571)

Elizabeth
(b. & d.1554)

Edward, Lord
Beauchamp
(1561–1612)

JAMES VI
KING OF SCOTLAND
JAMES I
KING OF ENGLAND
(1566–1625)
(see HOUSE OF STUART)

Kings and Queens of Scotland

The lineage of the Kings and Queens of Scotland shows the ancestry of James VI of Scotland (James I of England) and how he descends from Fergus the Great, who died in 501. The same line also features Lady Jean Lyon, daughter of King Robert II (1316–90), an ancestor of Queen Elizabeth The Queen Mother. (Only monarchs and dynastic lines are shown here.)

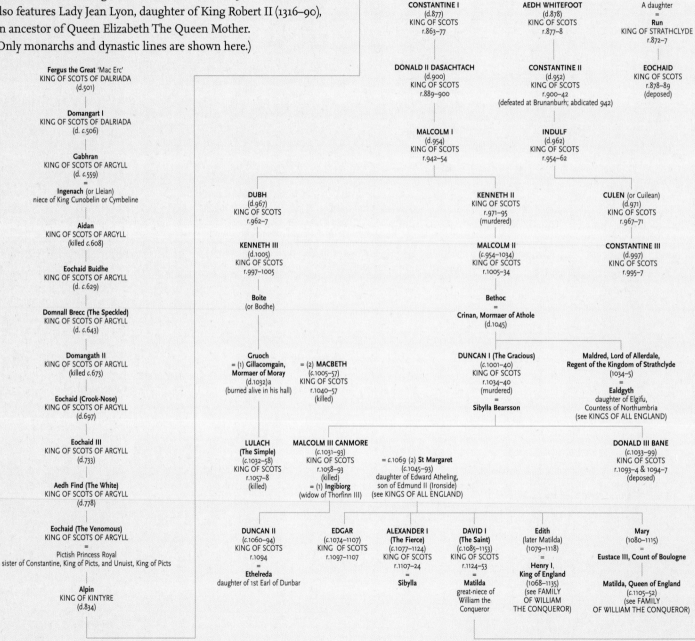

Fergus the Great 'Mac Erc'
KING OF SCOTS OF DALRIADA
(d.501)

Domangart I
KING OF SCOTS OF DALRIADA
(d. c.506)

Gabhran
KING OF SCOTS OF ARGYLL
(d. c.559)

Ingenach (or Lleian)
niece of King Cunobelin or Cymbeline

Aidan
KING OF SCOTS OF ARGYLL
(killed c.608)

Eochaid Buidhe
KING OF SCOTS OF ARGYLL
(d. c.629)

Domnall Brecc (The Speckled)
KING OF SCOTS OF ARGYLL
(d. c.643)

Domangath II
KING OF SCOTS OF ARGYLL
(killed c.673)

Eochaid (Crook-Nose)
KING OF SCOTS OF ARGYLL
(d.697)

Eochaid III
KING OF SCOTS OF ARGYLL
(d.733)

Aedh Find (The White)
KING OF SCOTS OF ARGYLL
(d.778)

Eochaid (The Venomous)
KING OF SCOTS OF ARGYLL
=
Pictish Princess Royal
sister of Constantine, King of Picts, and Unuist, King of Picts

Alpin
KING OF KINTYRE
(d.834)

KENNETH I MACALPIN
(d.859)
KING OF SCOTS
r.844–59

DONALD I
(d.863)
KING OF SCOTS
r.859–63

CONSTANTINE I
(d.877)
KING OF SCOTS
r.863–77

AEDH WHITEFOOT
(d.878)
KING OF SCOTS
r.877–8

A daughter
=
Run
KING OF STRATHCLYDE
r.872–7

DONALD II DASACHTACH
(d.900)
KING OF SCOTS
r.889–900

CONSTANTINE II
(d.952)
KING OF SCOTS
r.900–42
(defeated at Brunanburh; abdicated 942)

EOCHAID
KING OF SCOTS
r.878–89
(deposed)

MALCOLM I
(d.954)
KING OF SCOTS
r.942–54

INDULF
(d.962)
KING OF SCOTS
r.954–62

DUBH
(d.967)
KING OF SCOTS
r.962–7

KENNETH II
KING OF SCOTS
r.971–95
(murdered)

CULEN (or Cuilean)
(d.971)
KING OF SCOTS
r.967–71

KENNETH III
(d.1005)
KING OF SCOTS
r.997–1005

MALCOLM II
(c.954–1034)
KING OF SCOTS
r.1005–34

CONSTANTINE III
(d.997)
KING OF SCOTS
r.995–7

Boite
(or Bodhe)

Bethoc
=
Crinan, Mormaer of Athole
(d.1045)

Gruoch
= (1) **Gillacomgain,
Mormaer of Moray**
(d.1032)a
(burned alive in his hall)

= (2) **MACBETH**
(c.1005–57)
KING OF SCOTS
r.1040–57
(killed)

DUNCAN I (The Gracious)
(c.1001–40)
KING OF SCOTS
r.1034–40
(murdered)
=
Sibylla Bearsson

**Maldred, Lord of Allerdale,
Regent of the Kingdom of Strathclyde**
(1034–5)
=
Ealdgyth
daughter of Elgifu,
Countess of Northumbria
(see KINGS OF ALL ENGLAND)

**LULACH
(The Simple)**
(c.1032–58)
KING OF SCOTS
r.1057–8
(killed)

MALCOLM III CANMORE
(c.1031–93)
KING OF SCOTS
r.1058–93
(killed)
= (1) **Ingibiorg**
(widow of Thorfinn III)

= c.1069 (2) **St Margaret**
(c.1045–93)
daughter of Edward Atheling,
son of Edmund II (Ironside)
(see KINGS OF ALL ENGLAND)

DONALD III BANE
(c.1033–99)
KING OF SCOTS
r.1093–4 & 1094–7
(deposed)

DUNCAN II
(c.1060–94)
KING OF SCOTS
r.1094
=
Ethelreda
daughter of 1st Earl of Dunbar

EDGAR
(c.1074–1107)
KING OF SCOTS
r.1097–1107

**ALEXANDER I
(The Fierce)**
(c.1077–1124)
KING OF SCOTS
r.1107–24
=
Sibylla

**DAVID I
(The Saint)**
(c.1085–1153)
KING OF SCOTS
r.1124–53
=
Matilda
great-niece of
William the
Conqueror

Edith
(later Matilda)
(1079–1118)
=
**Henry I,
King of England**
(1068–1135)
(see FAMILY
OF WILLIAM
THE CONQUEROR)

Mary
(1080–1115)
=
Eustace III, Count of Boulogne

Matilda, Queen of England
(c.1105–52)
(see FAMILY
OF WILLIAM THE CONQUEROR)

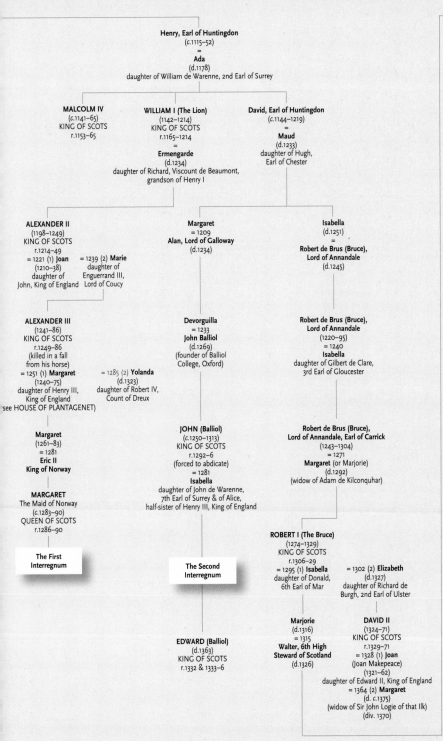

Henry, Earl of Huntingdon
(c.1115–52)
=
Ada
(d.1178)
daughter of William de Warenne, 2nd Earl of Surrey

MALCOLM IV
(c.1141–65)
KING OF SCOTS
r.1153–65

WILLIAM I (The Lion)
(1142–1214)
KING OF SCOTS
r.1165–1214
=
Ermengarde
(d.1234)
daughter of Richard, Viscount de Beaumont,
grandson of Henry I

David, Earl of Huntingdon
(c.1144–1219)
=
Maud
(d.1233)
daughter of Hugh,
Earl of Chester

ALEXANDER II
(1198–1249)
KING OF SCOTS
r.1214–49
= 1221 (1) **Joan**
(1210–38)
daughter of
John, King of England
= 1239 (2) **Marie**
daughter of
Enguerrand III,
Lord of Coucy

Margaret
= 1209
Alan, Lord of Galloway
(d.1234)

Isabella
(d.1251)
=
**Robert de Brus (Bruce),
Lord of Annandale**
(d.1245)

ALEXANDER III
(1241–86)
KING OF SCOTS
r.1249–86
(killed in a fall
from his horse)
= 1251 (1) **Margaret**
(1240–75)
daughter of Henry III,
King of England
(see HOUSE OF PLANTAGENET)
= 1285 (2) **Yolanda**
(d.1323)
daughter of Robert IV,
Count of Dreux

Devorguilla
= 1233
John Balliol
(d.1269)
(founder of Balliol
College, Oxford)

**Robert de Brus (Bruce),
Lord of Annandale**
(1220–95)
= 1240
Isabella
daughter of Gilbert de Clare,
3rd Earl of Gloucester

Margaret
(1261–83)
= 1281
**Eric II
King of Norway**

MARGARET
The Maid of Norway
(c.1283–90)
QUEEN OF SCOTS
r.1286–90

JOHN (Balliol)
(c.1250–1313)
KING OF SCOTS
r.1292–6
(forced to abdicate)
= 1281
Isabella
daughter of John de Warenne,
7th Earl of Surrey & of Alice,
half-sister of Henry III, King of England

**Robert de Brus (Bruce),
Lord of Annandale, Earl of Carrick**
(1243–1304)
= 1271
Margaret (or **Marjorie**)
(d.1292)
(widow of Adam de Kilconquhar)

The First
Interregnum

The Second
Interregnum

ROBERT I (The Bruce)
(1274–1329)
KING OF SCOTS
r.1306–29
= 1295 (1) **Isabella**
daughter of Donald,
6th Earl of Mar
= 1302 (2) **Elizabeth**
(d.1327)
daughter of Richard de
Burgh, 2nd Earl of Ulster

EDWARD (Balliol)
(d.1363)
KING OF SCOTS
r.1332 & 1333–6

Marjorie
(d.1316)
= 1315
**Walter, 6th High
Steward of Scotland**
(d.1326)

DAVID II
(1324–71)
KING OF SCOTS
r.1329–71
= 1328 (1) **Joan**
(Joan Makepeace)
(1321–62)
daughter of Edward II, King of England
= 1364 (2) **Margaret**
(d. c.1375)
(widow of Sir John Logie of that Ilk)
(div. 1370)

ROBERT II
(1316–90)
KING OF SCOTS
r.1371–90
= 1347 (1) **Elizabeth Mure**
(d. before 1355)
= 1355 (2) **Euphemia**
(d.1387)
(widow of John, 3rd Earl of Moray)

ROBERT III
(c.1337–1406)
KING OF SCOTS
r.1390–1406
= 1366/7
Annabella Drummond
(d.1401)

Jean
= (1) Sir John Keith
= (2) Sir John Lyon,
Chamberlain of Scotland
(c.1361–82)
(killed)
Ancestor of Queen Elizabeth
The Queen Mother
= 1384 (3) Sir James Sandilands
of Calder

JAMES I
(1394–1437)
KING OF SCOTS
r.1406–37
(assassinated)
= 1424
Joan Beaufort
(d.1445)
daughter of John,
Marquess of Dorset
& Somerset, KG

JAMES II
(1430–60)
KING OF SCOTS
r.1437–60
= 1449
Marie
(d.1463)
daughter of Arnold,
Duke of Gueldres

JAMES III
(1452–88)
KING OF SCOTS
r.1460–88
= 1469
Margaret
(d.1486)
daughter of Christian I,
King of Denmark

JAMES IV
(1473–1513)
KING OF SCOTS
r.1488–1513
= 1503
Margaret
(1489–1541)
daughter of Henry VII,
King of England
(see HOUSE OF TUDOR)

JAMES V
(1512–42)
KING OF SCOTS
r.1513–42
= 1537 (1) **Madeleine**
(1520–37)
daughter of Francis I,
King of France
= 1538 (2) **Marie**
(1515–60)
Regent of Scotland,
1554–60
(widow of Louis II,
duc de Longueville)

MARY
(1542–87)
QUEEN OF SCOTS
r.1542–67
(executed)
= 1558 (1) **Francis II**
King of France
(1544–60)
= 1565 (2) **Henry**
Stuart, Lord Darnley
(1545–67)
(murdered)
= 1567 (3)
**James, 4th
Earl of Bothwell**
(1536–78)

JAMES VI, KING OF SCOTLAND
r.1567–1625
JAMES I, KING OF ENGLAND
(see HOUSE OF STUART)

INTERREGNUMS

The First Interregnum lasted
from 1290 until 1292, when
Edward I, King of England,
pronounced at Berwick in
favour of John Balliol
(c.1250–1313), who was
crowned at Scone.

The Second Interregnum
began in 1296, when Edward I
took over the government and
proceeded to treat Scotland
as a conquered country. There
was then a long struggle for
independence. This was led
first by Sir William Wallace
(c.1270–1305) and then by
Robert Bruce (1274–1329).
The latter succeeded in
establishing himself as
Robert I in 1306; he was
crowned at Scone on 27 March.

House of Stuart

RIGHT
Paul van Somer
(c.1576–1621/2), *James I,*
*c.*1620.

James VI, King of Scotland, became James I of England in 1603 (r.1603–25), and the two countries shared a monarch thereafter. James was married to Anne of Denmark (1574–1619), who bore him nine children, three of whom survived infancy. James I's eldest son, Henry Frederick, Prince of Wales, predeceased him in 1612, so James was succeeded by his second son, who became Charles I. James I's daughter, Elizabeth (1596–1662), was the source of the Hanoverian succession. Her grandson was George I.

Charles I (r.1625–49) was a great patron of the arts, but his reign was overshadowed by his conflicts with Parliament. The dissolution of Parliament in 1629 was followed by 11 years of the King's personal rule. Civil war broke out in England in 1642, leading to the King's eventual defeat at the hands of Oliver Cromwell (1599–1658), in 1646. Charles I was executed in Whitehall in 1649, and the only break in the long monarchic succession then occurred, with England becoming a republic under Cromwell.

Parliament declared England to be a Commonwealth, and consigned the powers of government to a reformed House of Commons and a Council of State. In reality, power lay with the army and Cromwell, who

became Lord Protector in 1653. Oliver Cromwell died in 1658 and was buried in Westminster Abbey. (At the Restoration in 1660, his body was disinterred, dragged to Tyburn and beheaded; his head was stuck on a pike at Westminster, where it remained for 20 years.) His son, Richard Cromwell (1626–1712), was proclaimed Protector, but proved unfit to rule and abdicated in 1659.

Meanwhile, the future Charles II had escaped abroad. Following his father's execution, he returned with an army and was crowned King of Scotland at Scone, on 1 January 1651. He then marched to England, but was defeated by Cromwell at the battle of Worcester and fled into exile. In May 1660, Charles made a triumphant return to London.

Charles II (r.1660–85) had to work hard, particularly to mend the religious divisions created by his father. Royal powers and privileges had been severely limited by Parliament. This was a turning point in English history, as Parliament maintained a superior position to that of the King; and from the roots of the Cavaliers and Roundheads of the Civil War grew the concept of political parties as we know them today. Charles II fathered many illegitimate children and was the ancestor of two members of the British Royal Family:

OPPOSITE
Sir Anthony Van Dyck,
Charles I in three positions,
1635–6.

RIGHT
Pierre Mignard (1612–95),
The Family of James II,
1694.

THE BILL OF RIGHTS, 1689

In 1689, a convention of Parliament drew up a declaration that affirmed the rights and liberties of the people. The Bill of Rights received the royal assent on 16 December. The Bill made the sovereign subject to the laws of the land, and linked the succession to the acceptance by the new sovereign of the rights of the people. It is this Bill that excluded James II (who was still alive) and any of his descendants from succeeding to the throne. The Bill also prevented any Roman Catholics – or those married to Catholics – from ascending the throne. The throne was therefore offered not to James II's infant son, but to his impeccably Protestant daughter, Mary, and her husband, William of Orange, who accepted the Bill of Rights.

The sovereign was bound to agree, in the coronation oath, to govern 'according to the statutes of Parliament agreed upon and the laws and customs of the same'. The Bill ordained that parliaments were to be summoned frequently, and it made the monarch dependent on Parliament for funds – and thus established the guidelines for a successful constitutional monarchy.

Princess Alice, Duchess of Gloucester (Queen Elizabeth II's aunt, see page 60), and Diana, Princess of Wales (who had three lines of descent from Charles II). Charles II was a charismatic and pragmatic monarch. His otherwise successful reign was blighted by the Great Plague in 1665 and the Great Fire of London in 1666.

As Charles II had no legitimate children, in 1685 he was succeeded by his brother, James II (r.1685–8), who was a Catholic. James had married the Protestant Anne Hyde (1638–71), daughter of Charles II's Lord Chancellor, Lord Clarendon (1609–74). Their daughter, Mary, also a Protestant, was James's heir, and was married to her Dutch Protestant cousin, William, Prince of Orange, the Stadholder of the Netherlands.

In 1688, James II's Catholic second wife, Mary of Modena (1658–1718), gave birth to a son, giving rise to a genuine fear of a Catholic succession. William of Orange, professing himself Protector of the Protestant cause, was invited to come to England to battle against his father-in-law, James II, who had determined on a course to bring England back to Catholicism. Finding opposition on all sides, James II threw the Great Seal of England into the Thames and fled abroad, enabling William of Orange to seize the throne without bloodshed, ruling jointly with his wife, James II's daughter, as William III and Mary II (r.1689–94), and, after her death, as sole King of England and Scotland (r.1694–1702). This joint monarchy was unique in the history of Britain.

LEFT
Willem Wissing (1656–87), *Mary II, when Princess of Orange, c.*1685.

THE ACT OF SETTLEMENT, 1701

The Act of Settlement further limited the powers of the Crown and secured the rights and liberties of the people, and confirmed that it was for Parliament to determine the title to the throne. It followed in the wake of the Bill of Rights and its main purpose was to secure the Protestant succession. The Bill of Rights had provided that the Crown would pass to the heirs of Mary II, then to Queen Anne and her heirs, but neither Queen left surviving issue. There was a need to identify the rightful heir to the throne. Sophia, Electress of Hanover (1630–1714), niece of Charles I, and granddaughter of James I, was selected to succeed, being the next eligible Protestant in line. It was her son who succeeded as George I after Queen Anne's death, bypassing Catholic claimants to the throne.

The Act confirmed further conditions: the sovereign could not be a Roman Catholic or be married to a Catholic. He or she had to maintain the Church of England (and, following the Act of Union of 1707, the Church of Scotland). The sovereign was to be in communion with the Church of England, and had to promise to maintain the Protestant religion. Parliamentary consent was required for the sovereign to engage in war, and judges were made independent of 'the royal pleasure'. The Act marked another significant step towards the modern constitutional monarchy.

House of Stuart

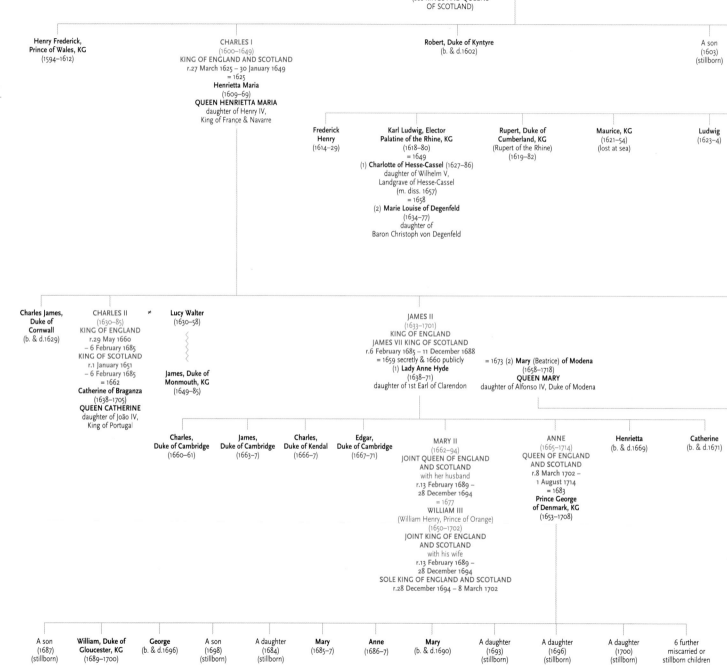

JAMES I
(1566–1625)
KING OF ENGLAND
r.24 March 1603 – 27 March 1625
JAMES VI
KING OF SCOTLAND
(see KINGS AND QUEENS
OF SCOTLAND)

= 1589

Anne of Denmark
(1574–1619)
QUEEN ANNE
daughter of Frederik II,
King of Denmark & Norway, KG

Henry Frederick,
Prince of Wales, KG
(1594–1612)

CHARLES I
(1600–1649)
KING OF ENGLAND AND SCOTLAND
r.27 March 1625 – 30 January 1649
= 1625
Henrietta Maria
(1609–69)
QUEEN HENRIETTA MARIA
daughter of Henry IV,
King of France & Navarre

Robert, Duke of Kyntyre
(b. & d.1602)

A son
(1603)
(stillborn)

Frederick
Henry
(1614–29)

Karl Ludwig, Elector
Palatine of the Rhine, KG
(1618–80)
= 1649
(1) Charlotte of Hesse-Cassel (1627–86)
daughter of Wilhelm V,
Landgrave of Hesse-Cassel
(m. diss. 1657)
= 1658
(2) Marie Louise of Degenfeld
(1634–77)
daughter of
Baron Christoph von Degenfeld

Rupert, Duke of
Cumberland, KG
(Rupert of the Rhine)
(1619–82)

Maurice, KG
(1621–54)
(lost at sea)

Ludwig
(1623–4)

Charles James,
Duke of
Cornwall
(b. & d.1629)

CHARLES II
(1630–85)
KING OF ENGLAND
r.29 May 1660
– 6 February 1685
KING OF SCOTLAND
r.1 January 1651
– 6 February 1685
= 1662
Catherine of Braganza
(1638–1705)
QUEEN CATHERINE
daughter of João IV,
King of Portugal

Lucy Walter
(1630–58)

James, Duke of
Monmouth, KG
(1649–85)

JAMES II
(1633–1701)
KING OF ENGLAND
JAMES VII KING OF SCOTLAND
r.6 February 1685 – 11 December 1688
= 1659 secretly & 1660 publicly
(1) **Lady Anne Hyde**
(1638–71)
daughter of 1st Earl of Clarendon

= 1673 (2) **Mary** (Beatrice) **of Modena**
(1658–1718)
QUEEN MARY
daughter of Alfonso IV, Duke of Modena

Charles,
Duke of Cambridge
(1660–61)

James,
Duke of Cambridge
(1663–7)

Charles,
Duke of Kendal
(1666–7)

Edgar,
Duke of Cambridge
(1667–71)

MARY II
(1662–94)
JOINT QUEEN OF ENGLAND
AND SCOTLAND
with her husband
r.13 February 1689 –
28 December 1694
= 1677
WILLIAM III
(William Henry, Prince of Orange)
(1650–1702)
JOINT KING OF ENGLAND
AND SCOTLAND
with his wife
r.13 February 1689 –
28 December 1694
SOLE KING OF ENGLAND AND SCOTLAND
r.28 December 1694 – 8 March 1702

ANNE
(1665–1714)
QUEEN OF ENGLAND
AND SCOTLAND
r.8 March 1702 –
1 August 1714
= 1683
**Prince George
of Denmark, KG**
(1653–1708)

Henrietta
(b. & d.1669)

Catherine
(b. & d.1671)

A son
(1687)
(stillborn)

**William, Duke of
Gloucester, KG**
(1689–1700)

George
(b. & d.1696)

A son
(1698)
(stillborn)

A daughter
(1684)
(stillborn)

Mary
(1685–7)

Anne
(1686–7)

Mary
(b. & d.1690)

A daughter
(1693)
(stillborn)

A daughter
(1696)
(stillborn)

A daughter
(1700)
(stillborn)

6 further
miscarried or
stillborn children

Elizabeth
(1596–1662)
= 1613
Frederick V
King of Bohemia, KG
and Elector Palatine of the Rhine
(1596–1632)

Margaret
(1598–1600)

Mary
(1605–7)

Sophia
(b. & d.1606)

1 further stillborn child

Edward, KG
(1624–63)
= 1645
Anne
(1616–84)
daughter of Charles,
Duke of Nevers & Mantua
(divorced wife of duc de Guise)

Philip
(1627–50)
(killed at Battle of
Rethel)

Gustavus
(1632–41)

Elizabeth
(1618–80)

Margaret
(1622–1709)

Henrietta Maria
(1626–51)
= 1651
Sigismund Rákóczy,
Prince of Siebenbürgen
(d.1652)

Charlotte
(1628–31)

Sophia
Heiress Presumptive,
1702–14
(1630–1714)
= 1658
Ernst August, Elector of Hanover
& Duke of Brunswick-Lüneburg & Zelle, KG
(1629–98)

GEORGE I
(1660–1727)
KING OF GREAT BRITAIN
(see FAMILY OF GEORGE I
AND GEORGE II)

Friedrich August
(1661–91)
(killed in battle)

Maximilian
(1666–1726)

A son
(1666)
(stillborn twin with
Maximilian)

Karl Philip
(1669–90)
(killed in battle)

Christian
(1671–1703)
(drowned in the
Danube)

**Ernst August,
Duke of York &
Albany**
(1674–1728)

Sophie Charlotte
(1668–1705)
= 1684
Frederick I
King in Prussia, KG
(1657–1713)
(as his second wife)

Henry, Duke of Gloucester, KG
(1640–60)

Mary
The Princess Royal
(1631–60)
= 1641
Willem II, Prince of Orange, KG
(d.1650)

Elizabeth
(1635–50)

Anne
(1637–40)

Catherine
(b. & d.1639)

Henrietta
(1644–70)
= 1661
**Philippe, Duke of
Orleans**
(1640–1701)

Friedrich Wilhelm I
King in Prussia
(1688–1740)
= 1706
Sophia Dorothea
(1687–1757)
daughter of King George I

**Charles, Duke of
Cambridge**
(b. & d.1677)

**James, Prince of
Wales, KG**
(1688–1766)
(The Old Pretender,
proclaimed
King James III in 1701)
= 1719
Clementina Sobieska
(1702–35)
daughter of
Prince Jakob Sobieski, son of
Jan III, King of Poland

Catherine
(b. & d.1675)

Isabella
(1676–81)

Charlotte
(b. & d.1682)

Louisa
(1692–1712)

William Henry,
Prince of Orange
(1650–1702)
KING WILLIAM III,
JOINT KING OF
ENGLAND AND
SCOTLAND

Charles Edward
(1720–88)
(Prince of Wales; Prince Regent in Scotland 1745;
Count of Albany; 'The Young Pretender',
recognised as Charles III by his adherents)
= 1772
Princess Louise of Stolberg-Gedern
(1752–1824)
daughter of Gustavus, Prince of Stolberg-Gedern

**Henry Benedict,
Duke of York, Cardinal
York**
(1725–1807)
(recognised as Henry IX
by his adherents)

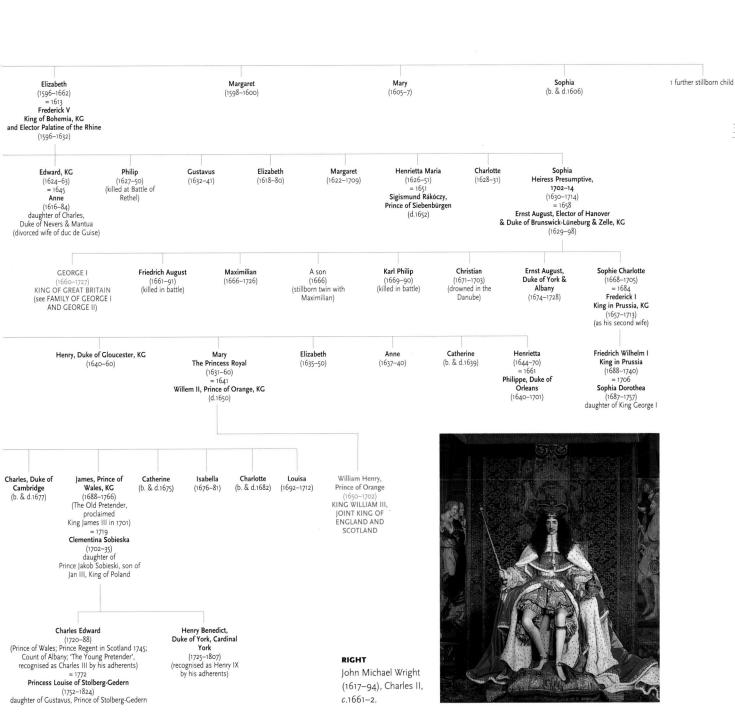

RIGHT
John Michael Wright
(1617–94), Charles II,
c.1661–2.

Mary II took little part in public affairs, and died, childless, in 1694. After William III's death, Mary II's sister, Anne (r.1702–14), began her reign. Tragically, of her many children, only one survived infancy, and he died at the age of 11. In the absence of an immediate successor, the Crown passed to George I, the first of the Hanoverian kings. His succession had been achieved by the Act of Settlement of 1701, which regulated the future descent of the Crown to ensure Protestant rule.

James II's children by his second wife, Mary of Modena, were raised as Catholics, but continued to claim the right of succession. On the death of James II, in 1701, James, Prince of Wales (1688–1766), known as 'the Old Pretender', was proclaimed King James III by his Jacobite supporters, and in 1715, he launched an unsuccessful uprising against George I.

LEFT
Charles Jervas
(c.1675–1739),
Queen Anne, 1710,
after Sir Godfrey Kneller.

RIGHT
After Sir Godfrey Kneller
(1646–1723), *William III*,
1700.

A second attempt, in 1745, by his son, Charles (1720–88), known as 'the Young Pretender', or 'Bonnie Prince Charlie', also failed. The male line of the Stuart family died out in 1807, with the death of Henry, Cardinal York (1725–1807). The heirs to the houses of Normandy (the family of William the Conqueror), Plantagenet, Tudor and Stuart claim their right of succession through Henrietta (1644–70), the youngest sister of Charles II and James II, though as Catholics they are debarred.

ACT OF UNION

On 6 March 1707, the Act of Union between England and Scotland was passed, and 'Great Britain' officially came into being. The royal style and title changed accordingly, so that the sovereign's realm encompassed 'Great Britain, France and Ireland'.

ns of Edward the Confessor

Arms of Edward III

Arms of Queen Anne

Arms of Harold II

Arms of Richard II

Arms of George I and George II

Arms of Henry III

Arms of Henry VI, Henry VII and Henry VIII

Arms of George III

Arms of Edward I

Arms of Charles I

Arms of Queen Victoria, King Edward VII
and the House of Windsor

Arms of Edward II

Arms of William III and Mary II

While earlier monarchs had arms attributed to them – most notably William I and his two golden lions – it was not until around 1198, during the reign of Richard I, that royal heraldry as we know it was officially recognised.

That first manifestation of official royal heraldry came in the form of the three golden lions on a red field. This changed in 1340, following Edward III's claim to the throne of France, which led to the arms of England being quartered with those of France, and the introduction of the fleur-de-lis. Save for a few minor alterations to the number of fleurs-de-lis during Henry IV's reign, this design continued until James I and VI's reign, when the Lion of Scotland and the Harp of Ireland were introduced.

When William III and Mary II were proclaimed joint Sovereigns in 1689, an inescutcheon of the arms of Nassau appeared in the centre of the royal arms. This was short-lived, however, and a further alteration took place in 1707, following the Act of Union with Scotland. This change was confined to the reign of Queen Anne, and with the throne passing to the Elector of Hanover in 1714, allusions to Hanover were incorporated into the royal arms.

This continued unchanged until 1801, when a more simplistic coat was adopted. On this occasion, the opportunity was taken to omit the arms of France and instead to display the arms of England (twice), Scotland and Ireland quarterly. The appearance of an inescutcheon with an electoral bonnet once again reflected the dynasty's German origins. The raising of Hanover to a kingdom in 1814 resulted in one further minor change, when the electoral bonnet turned into a crown.

The evolution of the royal arms reached its final stage of development with Queen Victoria's accession in 1837. Salic law prevented her succession to the kingdom of Hanover, so the crowned inescutcheon was dispensed with and the royal arms as we know them today emerged.

Family of George I and George II

The House of Hanover leads in direct and unbroken succession from George Louis, Elector of Hanover, to Queen Elizabeth II.

George Louis succeeded to the throne as George I (r.1714–27), under the terms of the Act of Settlement of 1701 (see page 37). Hanover (which became a kingdom in 1814) was thus joined to the British Crown, and remained so until 1837. Queen Victoria was unable to inherit the kingdom of Hanover, since a woman could not inherit if there was a male heir, and it passed instead to her uncle, the Duke of Cumberland. George I arrived in Britain in 1714, having divorced his wife for adultery in 1694. He never learned to speak English, was neither a popular nor an able king, and was in constant dispute with his son, the Prince of Wales. He died at Osnabrück in 1727.

George I was succeeded by George II (r.1727–60), who was born in Hanover. A more popular sovereign than his father, he was soundly advised by his wife, Caroline of Brandenburg-Ansbach (1683–1737), who played a greater role in affairs of state than most queens consort. George II's reign was largely peaceful, despite the second Jacobite Uprising of 1745, led by Bonnie Prince Charlie, James II's grandson.

George II's son, Frederick, Prince of Wales, died suddenly in 1751, so George II was succeeded by Frederick's son, as George III.

OPPOSITE LEFT
John Vanderbank (1694–1739), *George I*, 1726.

OPPOSITE RIGHT
Studio of John Shackleton (d.1767), *George II*, 1760–65.

RIGHT
William Hogarth (1697–1764), *The Family of George II*, c.1731–2.

GEORGE I
(1660–1727)
KING OF GREAT BRITAIN
AND IRELAND
r.1 August 1714 – 11 June 1727

= 1682

**Sophia Dorothea
of Brunswick-Lüneburg**
(1666–1726)
daughter of Georg Wilhelm,
Duke of Brunswick-Lüneburg & Zelle, KG
(never acknowledged as Queen of Great Britain)
(div. 1694)

GEORGE II
(1683–1760)
KING OF GREAT BRITAIN AND IRELAND
r.11 June 1727 – 25 October 1760
= 1705
Princess Caroline of Brandenburg-Ansbach
(1683–1737)
QUEEN CAROLINE
daughter of Johann Friedrich, Margrave
of Brandenburg-Ansbach

Sophia Dorothea
(1687–1757)
= 1706
Friedrich Wilhelm I
King in Prussia, KG
(1688–1740)
(see HOUSE OF STUART)

**Frederick,
Prince of Wales, KG**
(1707–51)
= 1736
**Princess Augusta of
Saxe-Gotha-Altenburg**
(1719–72)
daughter of HSH Friedrich II,
Duke of Saxe-Gotha-Altenburg

A son
(1716)
(stillborn)

George William
(1717–18)

**William,
Duke of Cumberland, KG**
(1721–65)

**Anne
The Princess Royal**
(1709–59)
= 1734
Willem IV, Prince of Orange, KG
(1711–51)

Amelia
(1711–86)

Caroline
(1713–57)

Mary
(1723–72)
= 1740
**Prince Friedrich II,
Landgrave of Hesse-Cassel, KG**
(1720–85)

Louisa
(1724–51)
= 1743
**Frederik V
King of Denmark**
(1723–66)

GEORGE III
(1738–1820)
KING OF GREAT BRITAIN
AND IRELAND (THE UNITED
KINGDOM)
(see FAMILY OF
GEORGE III)

**Edward,
Duke of York &
Albany, KG**
(1739–67)

**William,
Duke of Gloucester, KG**
(1743–1805)
= 1766
Maria, Countess Waldegrave
(1736–1807)
daughter of Hon. Sir Edward Walpole

**Henry,
Duke of Cumberland &
Strathearn, KG**
(1745–90)
= 1771
Hon. Anne Horton
(1743–1808)
daughter of 1st Baron Irnham
(widow of Christopher Horton)

Frederick
(1750–65)

Augusta
(1737–1813)
= 1764
**Karl II,
Duke of Brunswick, KG**
(1735–1806)

Elizabeth
(1740–59)

Louisa Anne
(1749–68)

Caroline Matilda
(1751–75)
= 1766
**Christian VII
King of Denmark**
(1749–1808)

**William,
2nd Duke of Gloucester, KG**
(1776–1834)
= 1816
Princess Mary
(1776–1857)
daughter of King George III
(see FAMILY OF GEORGE III)

Sophia Matilda
(1773–1844)

Caroline
(1774–5)

Family of George III

George III (r.1760–1820) was the first British-born king in the House of Hanover. His 60-year reign saw the American War of Independence (as a result of which Britain lost her colonies in America) and the Napoleonic Wars in Europe. George III was plagued by attacks of mental illness, now known to be porphyria. As a result, his son, the Prince of Wales, served as Regent, from 1811 until George III's death in 1820.

The Prince Regent succeeded as George IV (r.1820–30). He was an extravagant and extrovert figure, who converted Buckingham House into a stately palace, built the Royal Pavilion at Brighton, enlarged Carlton House in London and remodelled Windsor Castle. The Royal Marriages Act, passed during his father's reign, affected the new king. His marriage, in 1785, to the twice-widowed Roman Catholic, Mary Anne Fitzherbert (1756–1837),

LEFT
Johan Zoffany (1733/4–1810), *George III, Queen Charlotte and their six eldest children*, 1770.

THE ROYAL MARRIAGES ACT, 1772

The Royal Marriages Act of 1772 was passed because George III was displeased that two of his brothers – William, Duke of Gloucester (1743–1805) and Henry, Duke of Cumberland (1745–90) – had married commoners, without his knowledge or consent. It granted the sovereign some powers to prevent or delay unsuitable marriages involving the family, which were not legal without his consent.

The purpose of the Act was to reserve to the monarch the right to approve the marriages of any descendant of George II, other than the issue of princesses who married into foreign families. It stated: 'We have taken this weighty matter into our serious consideration; and being sensible that marriages in the royal family are of the highest importance to the state, and that therefore Kings of this realm have ever been entrusted with the care and approbation thereof.'

The Act decreed that the sovereign's permission was required to be signified 'under the great seal, and declared in council'. Any marriage or matrimonial contract entered into without such consent would be 'null and void, to all intents and purposes whatsoever'. There is one interesting proviso. When a member of the royal family reached the age of 25, he or she could give notice to the Privy Council of an intention to marry and, even if the sovereign's permission were withheld, after a year they would be free to marry, unless, within that year, 'both houses of parliament … expressly declare their disapprobation of such intended marriage'.

The Royal Marriages Act is still in force today, and all descendants of George II (other than those who also descend from someone who married into a foreign royal house) are bound by it.

had been declared null and void, and he was obliged to marry his cousin, Caroline of Brunswick (1768–1821), in 1795. This marriage was controversial and unsatisfactory (he even debarred his wife from the coronation), although it produced a daughter, Charlotte, in 1796. Charlotte married Prince Leopold of Saxe-Coburg-Saalfeld (1790–1865), but died in childbirth in 1817.

On Charlotte's death, the Prince Regent's surviving six brothers and five sisters were left in the line of succession to the throne. Two of the royal dukes were married, without legitimate children, three were

Family of George III

GEORGE III
(1738–1820)
KING OF THE UNITED KINGDOM OF
GREAT BRITAIN AND IRELAND
r.25 October 1760 – 29 January 1820

= 1761

Princess Charlotte
of Mecklenburg-Strelitz
(1744–1818)
QUEEN CHARLOTTE
daughter of Duke Karl of Mecklenburg-Strelitz

GEORGE IV
(1762–1830)
KING OF THE UNITED KINGDOM OF
GREAT BRITAIN AND IRELAND
Regent from 5 February 1811
r.29 January 1820
– 26 June 1830
= 1785
(1) **Mrs Mary Anne Fitzherbert** (1756–1837)
daughter of Walter Smythe
(in contravention of the Royal Marriages Act;
marriage declared null and void)
= 1795
(2) **Princess Caroline**
of Brunswick
(1768–1821)
(his 1st cousin)
daughter of Karl II, Duke of Brunswick, KG

Frederick,
Duke of York & Albany, KG
(1763–1827)
= 1791
Princess Frederica
of Prussia
(1767–1820)
daughter of
King Friedrich Wilhelm II of Prussia

WILLIAM IV
(1765–1837)
KING OF THE UNITED KINGDOM
OF GREAT BRITAIN AND
IRELAND
r.26 June 1830 – 20 June 1837
= 1818
Princess Adelaide
of Saxe-Meiningen
(1792–1849)
QUEEN ADELAIDE
daughter of
Duke Georg I of Saxe-Meiningen

Edward,
Duke of Kent, KG
(1767–1820)
= 1818
Princess Victoria
(The Duchess of Kent)
(1786–1861)
daughter of Prince Franz,
Duke of Saxe-Coburg-Saalfeld
(widow of Prince Emich Karl
of Leiningen)

Ernest Augustus,
Duke of Cumberland, KG
(1771–1851)
(Ernst August,
King of Hanover from 1837)
= 1815
Princess Frederica
(1778–1841)
daughter of Prince Karl,
Duke of Mecklenburg-Strelitz
(widow of Prince Friedrich of
Solms-Braunfels, &
of Prince Ludwig of Prussia)

Charlotte
(b. & d.1819)

Elizabeth
(1820–21)

ALEXANDRINA VICTORIA
(1819–1901)
QUEEN VICTORIA
QUEEN OF THE UNITED KINGDOM
OF GREAT BRITAIN AND IRELAND,
EMPRESS OF INDIA
(see FAMILY OF QUEEN VICTORIA)

Georg V
King of Hanover, KG
(1819–78)
(lost throne of Hanover to Prussia, 1866)
= 1843
Princess Marie of Saxe-Altenburg
(1818–1907)
daughter of Duke Joseph of Saxe-Altenburg

Charlotte of Wales
Heiress Presumptive
(1796–1817)
= 1816
Prince Leopold of
Saxe-Coburg-Saalfeld, KG
(1790–1865)
(later Leopold I,
King of the Belgians)

A son
(1817)
(stillborn)

ABOVE
Sir William Beechey
(1753–1839), *George IV*
when Prince of Wales, 1803.

Ernst August, Crown Prince
of Hanover,
3rd Duke of Cumberland, KG
(1845–1923)
= 1878
Princess Thyra of Denmark
(1853–1933)
daughter of King Christian IX of
Denmark, KG

from whom descend the present
royal House of Hanover, and the
royal family of Greece

Frederica
(1848–1926)
= 1880
Baron Alfons von
Pawel-Rammingen
(1843–1932)

Victoria von
Pawel-Rammingen
(b. & d.1881)

Marie
(1849–1904)

George, 2nd Marquess of Cambridge
(1895–1981)
= 1923
Dorothy Hastings
Marchioness of Cambridge
(1899–1988)
daughter of Hon. Osmond Hastings

Lady Mary Cambridge
(1924–1999)
=
Peter Whitley
(1923–2003)

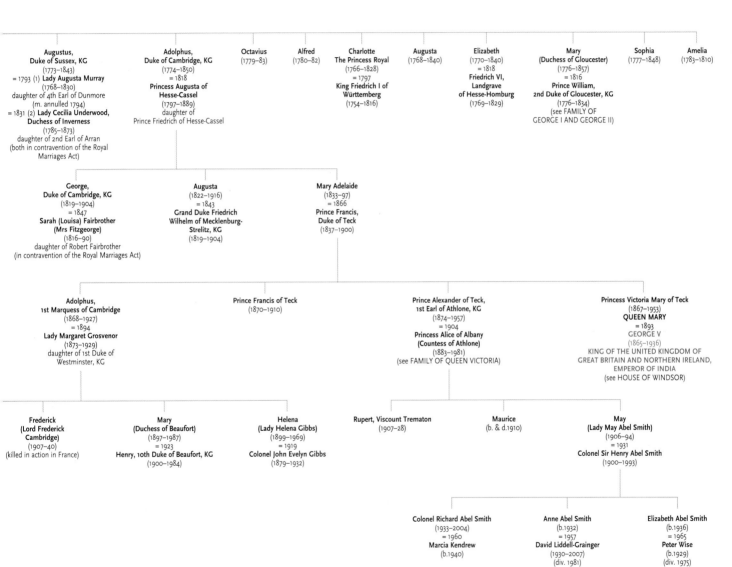

Augustus,
Duke of Sussex, KG
(1773–1843)
= 1793 (1) **Lady Augusta Murray**
(1768–1830)
daughter of 4th Earl of Dunmore
(m. annulled 1794)
= 1831 (2) **Lady Cecilia Underwood,**
Duchess of Inverness
(1785–1873)
daughter of 2nd Earl of Arran
(both in contravention of the Royal
Marriages Act)

Adolphus,
Duke of Cambridge, KG
(1774–1850)
= 1818
Princess Augusta of
Hesse-Cassel
(1797–1889)
daughter of
Prince Friedrich of Hesse-Cassel

Octavius
(1779–83)

Alfred
(1780–82)

Charlotte
The Princess Royal
(1766–1828)
= 1797
King Friedrich I of
Württemberg
(1754–1816)

Augusta
(1768–1840)

Elizabeth
(1770–1840)
= 1818
Friedrich VI,
Landgrave
of Hesse-Homburg
(1769–1829)

Mary
(Duchess of Gloucester)
(1776–1857)
= 1816
Prince William,
2nd Duke of Gloucester, KG
(1776–1834)
(see FAMILY OF
GEORGE I AND GEORGE II)

Sophia
(1777–1848)

Amelia
(1783–1810)

George,
Duke of Cambridge, KG
(1819–1904)
= 1847
Sarah (Louisa) Fairbrother
(Mrs Fitzgeorge)
(1816–90)
daughter of Robert Fairbrother
(in contravention of the Royal Marriages Act)

Augusta
(1822–1916)
= 1843
Grand Duke Friedrich
Wilhelm of Mecklenburg-
Strelitz, KG
(1819–1904)

Mary Adelaide
(1833–97)
= 1866
Prince Francis,
Duke of Teck
(1837–1900)

Adolphus,
1st Marquess of Cambridge
(1868–1927)
= 1894
Lady Margaret Grosvenor
(1873–1929)
daughter of 1st Duke of
Westminster, KG

Prince Francis of Teck
(1870–1910)

Prince Alexander of Teck,
1st Earl of Athlone, KG
(1874–1957)
= 1904
Princess Alice of Albany
(Countess of Athlone)
(1883–1981)
(see FAMILY OF QUEEN VICTORIA)

Princess Victoria Mary of Teck
(1867–1953)
QUEEN MARY
= 1893
GEORGE V
(1865–1936)
KING OF THE UNITED KINGDOM OF
GREAT BRITAIN AND NORTHERN IRELAND,
EMPEROR OF INDIA
(see HOUSE OF WINDSOR)

Frederick
(Lord Frederick
Cambridge)
(1907–40)
(killed in action in France)

Mary
(Duchess of Beaufort)
(1897–1987)
= 1923
Henry, 10th Duke of Beaufort, KG
(1900–1984)

Helena
(Lady Helena Gibbs)
(1899–1969)
= 1919
Colonel John Evelyn Gibbs
(1879–1932)

Rupert, Viscount Trematon
(1907–28)

Maurice
(b. & d.1910)

May
(Lady May Abel Smith)
(1906–94)
= 1931
Colonel Sir Henry Abel Smith
(1900–1993)

Colonel Richard Abel Smith
(1933–2004)
= 1960
Marcia Kendrew
(b.1940)

Anne Abel Smith
(b.1932)
= 1957
David Liddell-Grainger
(1930–2007)
(div. 1981)

Elizabeth Abel Smith
(b.1936)
= 1965
Peter Wise
(b.1929)
(div. 1975)

unmarried, and one had been married in contravention of the Royal Marriages Act. This situation created much concern, and thus, within about two months of each other, in 1818, the three bachelor princes married. One of them, Edward, Duke of Kent (1767–1820), produced an heir, the future Queen Victoria, in 1819.

The second son of George III was Frederick, Duke of York, who died, childless, in 1827. George IV was therefore succeeded by his next brother, William IV (r.1830–37), known as the 'sailor' King, due to his time in the navy before the accession. William IV had two legitimate daughters, who both died young.

George III's family tree also contains many of the descendants of Adolphus, Duke of Cambridge (1774–1850). Adolphus had a son and two daughters, the younger of whom, Mary Adelaide (1833–97), was married to the Duke of Teck (1837–1900), and was the mother of Princess Victoria Mary (Princess May) (1867–1953). In 1891, Princess May was engaged to Albert Victor, the Duke of Clarence and Avondale (1864–92), the second in direct line of succession to Queen Victoria. After his death early the following year, Princess May married the new heir, George, Duke of York; they became King George V and Queen Mary.

Thus Queen Elizabeth II has dual descent from George III, through the Duke of Kent and the Duke of Cambridge.

Family of Queen Victoria

During her long reign, Queen Victoria (r.1837–1901) established herself as a highly respected monarch, very different from her Hanoverian forebears. Her marriage to Prince Albert of Saxe-Coburg and Gotha (1819–61), in 1840, brought his powerful influence to the court.

Prince Albert's death, in 1861, left the Queen bereft, and during the middle years

ROYAL TITLES: OTHER ROYAL DUKEDOMS

The dukedom of Clarence has always been royal, and was conferred on George, brother of Edward IV; on the son of George III, who became William IV; and on the eldest son of Albert Edward, Prince of Wales (later King Edward VII), Prince Albert Victor, who died in 1892. There have been dukes of Albany, of whom the last holder was Charles Edward, a grandson of Queen Victoria. During the First World War, he was struck from the roll of peers, as was the Duke of Cumberland, on account of German connections. The dukedom of Cambridge was revived as a marquessate for Queen Mary's brother, but died out in 1981. It was revived again for Prince William of Wales on his marriage in 2011. The dukedom of Connaught, held by Queen Victoria's third son, Prince Arthur, died out with his grandson, in 1943. There have also been dukes of Kendal and Sussex.

ABOVE
Franz Xaver Winterhalter (1805–73), *The Royal Family in 1846*, 1846. The painting shows Queen Victoria and Prince Albert with their elder children, Alfred, Duke of Edinburgh, Albert Edward, Prince of Wales (later King Edward VII), Alice (later Grand Duchess of Hesse), Helena (later Princess Christian of Schleswig-Holstein) and Victoria (the future Empress Frederick of Germany).

of her reign she was seldom seen in public. Victoria became Empress of India in 1877, and by the time of her Golden Jubilee, in 1887, and her Diamond Jubilee, in 1897, she had become a much-revered monarch at the centre of a huge Empire.

Prince Albert predeceased his childless elder brother, Ernst II, Duke of Saxe-Coburg and Gotha (1818–93), which meant that one of his and Queen Victoria's sons would have to succeed their uncle in Coburg. The Prince of Wales renounced his claim to the duchy and the succession passed to his next brother, Alfred, Duke of Edinburgh (1844–1900), who became Duke of Saxe-Coburg and Gotha in 1893. His son, Alfred, predeceased him, and, in 1900, the next heir was Arthur, Duke of Connaught (1850–1942), followed by his son, Prince Arthur of Connaught (1883–1938). Both father and son made it clear that they did not wish to reside in Coburg; they were strongly supported by Queen Victoria, and the Coburg succession passed to the son of Prince Leopold, Duke of Albany (1853–84). Prince Charles Edward, 2nd Duke of Albany (1884–1954), became Duke of Saxe-Coburg and Gotha. He found himself on the 'enemy' side in the First World War, and was eventually stripped of his English dukedom and subsidiary titles. In 1915, he was also struck from the roll of the Order of the Garter. Before the Second World War, he became involved with the Nazi party, and he

was imprisoned at the end of the war. He died, a broken man, in 1954.

Had it not been for the Coburg succession, Charles Edward's descendants might have been brought up in England and served as minor members of the British royal family. As it is, his daughter, Sibylla (1908–72), was the mother of the present King of Sweden, Carl XVI Gustaf (b.1946). Many European royal families descend from Queen Victoria, including those of Sweden, Denmark, Norway and Spain, and the erstwhile royal houses of Germany, Russia, Greece and Romania. Kaiser Wilhelm II (1859–1941) was the son of Queen Victoria's eldest daughter, Victoria, Empress Frederick of Germany (1840–1901).

BELOW
Heinrich von Angeli
(1840–1925),
Queen Victoria, 1899.

LEFT
Queen Victoria holds her great-grandson, Prince Edward of York (the future Edward VIII), at his christening on 16 July 1894. Standing behind are Alexandra, Princess of Wales, the Prince's grandmother, and his mother, Victoria Mary, Duchess of York.

OPPOSITE
Sir George Hayter
(1792–1871),
Queen Victoria, 1840.
The Queen is depicted in her coronation robes.

Family of Queen Victoria

VICTORIA
(1819–1901)
QUEEN OF THE UNITED KINGDOM
OF GREAT BRITAIN AND IRELAND,
EMPRESS OF INDIA
r.20 June 1837 – 22 January 1901

= 1840

Prince Albert
of Saxe-Coburg & Gotha
(1819–61)
THE PRINCE CONSORT, KG

EDWARD VII
(1841–1910)
KING OF THE UNITED KINGDOM
OF GREAT BRITAIN AND IRELAND,
EMPEROR OF INDIA
(see HOUSE OF SAXE-COBURG & GOTHA)

Alfred,
Duke of Edinburgh, KG
(Duke of Saxe-Coburg & Gotha)
(1844–1900)
= 1874
Grand Duchess Marie of Russia
(1853–1920)
daughter of
Emperor Alexander II of Russia, KG

Arthur,
Duke of Connaught, KG
(1850–1942)
= 1879
Princess Louise Margaret of Prussia
(1860–1917)
daughter of
Prince Friedrich Karl of Prussia

Leopold,
Duke of Albany, KG
(1853–84)
= 1882
Princess Helen of Waldeck & Pyrmont
(1861–1922)
daughter of Georg Viktor,
Prince of Waldeck & Pyrmont

Alfred, KG
(1874–99)

Marie
(Queen of Romania)
(1875–1938)
= 1893
Ferdinand
King of Romania, KG
(1865–1927)

Victoria Melita
(1876–1936)
= 1894
(1) **Grand Duke**
Ernst Ludwig of Hesse
(1868–1937)
(div. 1901)
= 1905
(2) **Grand Duke**
Kirill of Russia
(1876–1938)

Alexandra
(1878–1942)
= 1896
Ernst,
7th Prince of Hohenlohe
Langenburg
(1863–1950)

Beatrice
(1884–1966)
= 1909
Prince Alfonso,
Infante of Spain
(1886–1975)

Arthur, KG
(Prince Arthur of
Connaught)
(1883–1938)
= 1913
Princess Alexandra,
Duchess of Fife
(1891–1959)
(see HOUSE OF
SAXE-COBURG &
GOTHA)

Margaret
(1882–1920)
= 1905
Crown Prince
Gustaf Adolf
of Sweden
(later Gustaf VI Adolf,
King of Sweden, KG)
(1882–1973)

Patricia
(Lady Patricia Ramsay)
(1886–1974)
= 1919
Admiral Hon.
Sir Alexander Ramsay
(1881–1972)

Charles Edward,
2nd Duke of Albany
(later Duke of
Saxe-Coburg & Gotha)
(1884–1954)
= 1905
Princess Victoria of
Schleswig-Holstein-
Sonderburg-Glücksburg
(1885–1970)
daughter of Friedrich,
Duke of Schleswig-Holstein-
Sonderburg-Glücksburg

Alice
(Princess Alice,
Countess of Athlone)
(1883–1981)
= 1904
Prince Alexander
of Teck,
Earl of Athlone, KG
(1874–1957)
(see FAMILY
OF GEORGE III)

Carol II
King of Romania, KG
(1893–1953)

Captain Alexander
Ramsay of Mar
(1919–2000)
= 1956
Hon. Flora Fraser,
now Lady Saltoun
(b.1930)

descendants

from whom
descend the royal
families of Sweden
& Denmark

from whom
descend the royal
family of Sweden
and the present
House of Saxe-
Coburg & Gotha

descendants

from whom descends the
present royal family of
Romania

BELOW
Roger Fenton (1819–69), *Queen Victoria,*
Prince Albert, and eight of their children,
photographed in the garden at Buckingham
Palace, 22 May 1854 (detail).

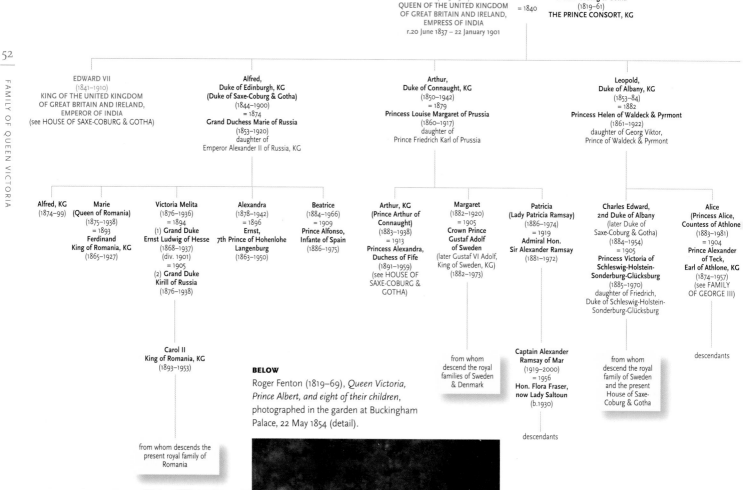

Victoria
The Princess Royal
(Empress Frederick)
(1840–1901)
= 1858
Emperor Frederick III,
German Emperor &
King of Prussia, KG
(1831–88)

Alice
(Grand Duchess of Hesse & by Rhine)
(1843–78)
= 1862
Ludwig IV,
Grand Duke of Hesse & by Rhine, KG
(1837–92)
(see ANCESTRY OF
HRH THE DUKE OF EDINBURGH)

Helena
(Princess Christian)
(1846–1923)
= 1866
Prince Christian
of Schleswig-Holstein-
Sonderburg-
Augustenburg, KG
(1831–1917)

Louise
(The Princess Louise,
Duchess of Argyll)
(1848–1939)
= 1871
John, 9th Duke of Argyll, KG
(1845–1914)

Beatrice
(1857–1944)
= 1885
Prince Henry of
Battenberg, KG
(1858–96)

Kaiser
Wilhelm II, KG
(1859–1941)

Christian Victor
(1867–1900)
(killed in Boer War)

Albert, Duke
of Schleswig-
Holstein-Sonderburg-
Augustenburg
(1869–1931)

Harald
(b. & d.1876)

A son
(1877)
(stillborn)

Helena
Victoria
(1870–1948)

Marie Louise
(1872–1956)
= 1891
Prince Aribert
of Anhalt
(1864–1933)
(annulled 1900)

Alexander,
Marquess of Carisbrooke
(1886–1960)
= 1917
Lady Irene Denison
(Marchioness of
Carisbrooke)
(1890–1956)
daughter of
2nd Earl of Londesborough

Leopold
(Lord Leopold
Mountbatten)
(1889–1922)

Maurice
(Prince Maurice of
Battenberg)
(1891–1914)
(died of wounds in
retreat from Mons)

Victoria Eugénie
(Queen of Spain)
(1887–1969)
= 1906
Alfonso XIII
King of Spain, KG
(1886–1941)

from Empress
Frederick descend
the royal families of
Prussia & Greece

Lady Iris Mountbatten
(1920–82)
(m. three times)

from whom
descends the royal
family of Spain

descendants

ABOVE
Laurits Regner Tuxen (1853–1927), *The Family of*
Queen Victoria in 1887, 1887. Painted at Windsor
Castle, Queen Victoria is surrounded by her
descendants and their spouses, at the time of
the Golden Jubilee. The little girl in the centre
foreground was to be the last surviving grandchild
of the Queen – Princess Alice, Countess of Athlone
(1883–1981), who lived to the age of 97.

House of Saxe-Coburg and Gotha

In 1901, King Edward VII (r.1901–10) became the first king of the House of Saxe-Coburg and Gotha, the family name of his father, Prince Albert, the Prince Consort.

For his first 60 years, as Prince of Wales, Edward had been prevented from participating in affairs of state. Although he undertook an increasing number of official duties, he was widely perceived as being indolent and pleasure-loving. Yet, when he became King, at the age of 59, he proved extremely popular with his subjects. His skill for diplomacy and foreign affairs helped to achieve the Entente Cordiale with France, in 1904.

In 1863, the future King Edward VII had married Princess Alexandra of Denmark (1844–1925). They had three sons and three daughters. Their eldest son, Albert Victor, Duke of Clarence, died, unmarried, in 1892, so the succession passed to the Duke of York, who succeeded to the throne as King George V.

King Edward VII's eldest daughter, Princess Louise (1867–1931), married the Duke of Fife (1849–1912) and had two daughters, Alexandra (known as Princess Arthur of Connaught; also Duchess of Fife in her own right) (1891–1959) and Maud (1893–1945). Princess Arthur of Connaught's son and heir, Alastair, 2nd Duke of Connaught (1914–43), predeceased her. Princess Maud had married Lord Carnegie, later Earl of Southesk (1893–1992). She also died before Alexandra, and the Dukedom of Fife passed to her son, James, the present Duke of Fife (b.1929).

King Edward VII's youngest daughter, Maud (1869–1938), married Prince Charles of Denmark (1872–1957), who was elected King of Norway in 1905 and took the name Haakon VII. Their son, Olav V (1903–91), was a regular visitor to Britain, and his descendants include the present King of Norway, Harald V (b.1937). King Edward's second daughter, Princess Victoria (1868–1935), remained unmarried.

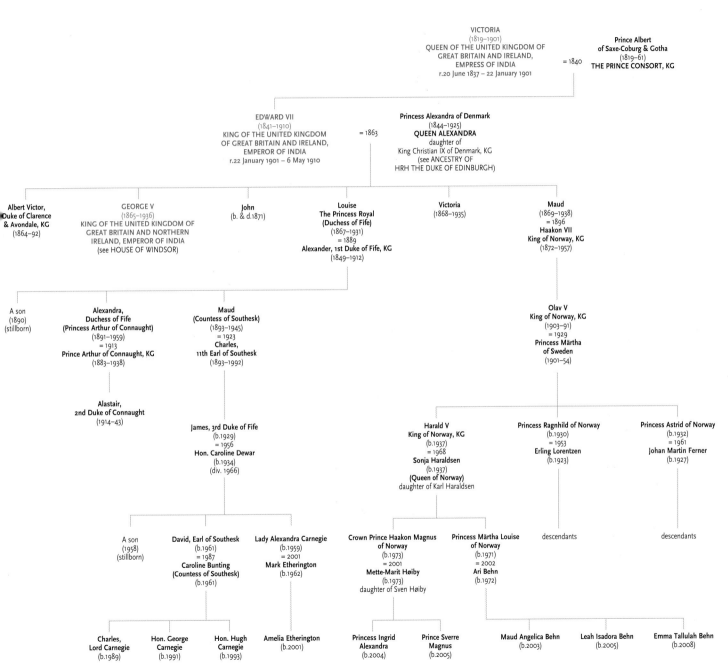

VICTORIA
(1819–1901)
QUEEN OF THE UNITED KINGDOM OF
GREAT BRITAIN AND IRELAND,
EMPRESS OF INDIA
r.20 June 1837 – 22 January 1901

= 1840

Prince Albert
of Saxe-Coburg & Gotha
(1819–61)
THE PRINCE CONSORT, KG

EDWARD VII
(1841–1910)
KING OF THE UNITED KINGDOM
OF GREAT BRITAIN AND IRELAND,
EMPEROR OF INDIA
r.22 January 1901 – 6 May 1910

= 1863

Princess Alexandra of Denmark
(1844–1925)
QUEEN ALEXANDRA
daughter of
King Christian IX of Denmark, KG
(see ANCESTRY OF
HRH THE DUKE OF EDINBURGH)

Albert Victor,
Duke of Clarence
& Avondale, KG
(1864–92)

GEORGE V
(1865–1936)
KING OF THE UNITED KINGDOM OF
GREAT BRITAIN AND NORTHERN
IRELAND, EMPEROR OF INDIA
(see HOUSE OF WINDSOR)

John
(b. & d.1871)

Louise
The Princess Royal
(Duchess of Fife)
(1867–1931)
= 1889
Alexander, 1st Duke of Fife, KG
(1849–1912)

Victoria
(1868–1935)

Maud
(1869–1938)
= 1896
Haakon VII
King of Norway, KG
(1872–1957)

A son
(1890)
(stillborn)

Alexandra,
Duchess of Fife
(Princess Arthur of Connaught)
(1891–1959)
= 1913
Prince Arthur of Connaught, KG
(1883–1938)

Maud
(Countess of Southesk)
(1893–1945)
= 1923
Charles,
11th Earl of Southesk
(1893–1992)

Olav V
King of Norway, KG
(1903–91)
= 1929
Princess Märtha
of Sweden
(1901–54)

Alastair,
2nd Duke of Connaught
(1914–43)

James, 3rd Duke of Fife
(b.1929)
= 1956
Hon. Caroline Dewar
(b.1934)
(div. 1966)

Harald V
King of Norway, KG
(b.1937)
= 1968
Sonja Haraldsen
(b.1937)
(Queen of Norway)
daughter of Karl Haraldsen

Princess Ragnhild of Norway
(b.1930)
= 1953
Erling Lorentzen
(b.1923)

Princess Astrid of Norway
(b.1932)
= 1961
Johan Martin Ferner
(b.1927)

A son
(1958)
(stillborn)

David, Earl of Southesk
(b.1961)
= 1987
Caroline Bunting
(Countess of Southesk)
(b.1961)

Lady Alexandra Carnegie
(b.1959)
= 2001
Mark Etherington
(b.1962)

Crown Prince Haakon Magnus
of Norway
(b.1973)
= 2001
Mette-Marit Høiby
(b.1973)
daughter of Sven Høiby

Princess Märtha Louise
of Norway
(b.1971)
= 2002
Ari Behn
(b.1972)

descendants

descendants

Charles,
Lord Carnegie
(b.1989)

Hon. George
Carnegie
(b.1991)

Hon. Hugh
Carnegie
(b.1993)

Amelia Etherington
(b.2001)

Princess Ingrid
Alexandra
(b.2004)

Prince Sverre
Magnus
(b.2005)

Maud Angelica Behn
(b.2003)

Leah Isadora Behn
(b.2005)

Emma Tallulah Behn
(b.2008)

House of Windsor

King George V (r.1910–36) married Princess Victoria Mary (May) of Teck, who was a descendant of George III through her mother, Princess Mary Adelaide, daughter of Adolphus, Duke of Cambridge. King George V's reign witnessed a number of constitutional crises and the trauma of the First World War. It was as the result of anti-German feelings towards members of the Royal House that King George V dropped the German style of the House of Saxe-Coburg (or Wettin, as the family name was sometimes known).

On 17 July 1917, George V declared, by royal proclamation, that 'Our House and Family shall be styled and known as the House and Family of Windsor.' Subsequently it was stated that 'the titles of Prince and Princess will be confined to the children and grandchildren of the Sovereign. The titles of Highness and Serene Highness will be allowed to die out and the use of "Royal Highness" will be confined to the children of the Sovereign and the children of the Sovereign's sons.' It added that 'in the third generation in the male line the younger sons will assume the family name of "Windsor" with the courtesy title of "Younger Sons of a Duke".'

Simultaneously, a number of relatives relinquished their German titles and assumed English ones. Queen Mary's eldest brother, Prince Adolphus, the Duke of Teck (1868–1927), became the Marquess of Cambridge, while her youngest brother, Alexander, became the Earl of Athlone (1874–1957). The daughters of Princess Christian (1846–1923) dropped the style 'of Schleswig-Holstein', and the Battenberg descendants of Princesses Beatrice (1857–1944) and Alice (1843–78) took the surname of Mountbatten; Prince Louis of Battenberg

(1854–1921) became the Marquess of Milford Haven, and Princess Beatrice's son, Alexander of Battenberg (1886–1960), became Marquess of Carisbrooke.

The direct effect of the King's proclamation was that the sons of his daughter, Princess Mary (1897–1965), would receive no title from their mother, whereas the daughters of Princess Louise, King Edward VII's eldest daughter, had been given titles in their own right.

This arrangement continued until 1952, when Queen Elizabeth II came to the throne. In the normal course of the succession, the style of Windsor would have had to change to that of the royal consort. The Earl Mountbatten of Burma – Prince Philip's uncle – assumed that the House of Mountbatten now ruled in Britain. This did not appeal either to Queen Mary or to the Prime Minister, Winston Churchill (1874–1965), who prevailed upon The Queen to declare, in April 1952, that 'She and her children shall be styled and known as the House and Family of Windsor, and that Her

ROYAL TITLES: PRINCESS ROYAL

The title of Princess Royal is reserved for the eldest daughter of the sovereign, and is held for life. It is granted by royal declaration, and is not a creation, like the dukedoms. There have been seven princesses royal to date. (Dates of declaration are shown in brackets.)

Princess Mary, daughter of Charles I (date of declaration unknown)
Princess Anne, daughter of George II (1727)
Princess Charlotte, daughter of George III,
the future Queen of Württemberg (1789)
Princess Victoria, daughter of Queen Victoria,
later Empress Frederick of Germany (1841)
Princess Louise, Duchess of Fife, daughter of King Edward VII (1905)
Princess Mary, Countess of Harewood,
daughter of King George V (1932)
Princess Anne, daughter of Queen Elizabeth II (1987)

ABOVE
Zara Phillips, The Queen and The Princess Royal
on horseback at Windsor, 10 April 2004.

HOUSE OF WINDSOR

Counsellors of State are appointed to execute the functions of the sovereign in the absence of the reigning king or queen, especially when abroad. For example, when Henry V and William III were abroad fighting, and when George I was in Hanover, each appointed a Guardian of the Realm, or *Custos Regni*.

King George V appointed Counsellors of State when he went to India in 1911–12, and when he was ill in 1928–9. Modern-day Counsellors of State are appointed by letters patent, under the terms of the Regency Acts, of which there have been three, in 1937, 1943 and 1953. They are appointed for a limited period of time and for a specific reason.

Under the Regency Acts, the Counsellors are the spouse of the sovereign and the next four in line to the throne who have reached the age of 21 (or 18 in the case of the heir apparent). At present, the Counsellors of State are The Duke of Edinburgh, The Prince of Wales, The Duke of Cambridge, Prince Henry of Wales and The Duke of York.

Counsellors of State are empowered to hold Privy Councils and signify The Queen's approval in Council, to issue commissions for giving the royal assent to Acts of Parliament (with the exception of Acts that affect royal styles or the Act of Settlement), to approve and sign proclamations, warrants and other such documents, and to exercise the royal prerogative and other statutory powers enabling The Queen to act for the safety and good government of the United Kingdom and colonies.

Counsellors are specifically not allowed to dissolve Parliament (other than on the express command of the sovereign), or to grant titles, ranks or dignities in the peerage. They are allowed to refuse to act if it appears to them that they should take specific instruction from the sovereign. Usually, two Counsellors act together.

In their time, members of the Royal Family such as Princess Margaret (1930–2002), Prince Henry, Duke of Gloucester (1900–74), Princess Mary, the late Princess Royal, and even Princess Arthur of Connaught and the Countess of Southesk (granddaughters of King Edward VII) all acted as Counsellors of State, as did the 7th Earl of Harewood (1923–2011) when a young man, all owing to their position in line of succession to the throne.

BELOW
After ten weeks with his regiment on the front line in Afghanistan in 2008, Prince Harry was welcomed home by Prince Charles and Prince William at RAF Brize Norton. All three are Counsellors of State.

ABOVE
Sir Gerald Kelly (1879–1972), *King George VI*, 1938–45. This portrait, showing the King in his coronation robes, was commissioned in 1938 and kept Sir Gerald at work at Windsor Castle throughout the Second World War.

ROYAL TITLES: THE DUKE OF EDINBURGH

Frederick, eldest son of George, Prince of Wales (later George II), was the first Duke of Edinburgh, in 1726. The dukedom merged with the Crown on the succession, in 1760, of George III, who gave it as a second dukedom to the Duke of Gloucester in 1764. The title died out, to be revived by Queen Victoria for her second son, Prince Alfred, in 1866. After his death, in 1900, the title again became extinct. King George VI conferred it on Lieutenant Philip Mountbatten, RN, when he married Princess Elizabeth, in 1947.

descendants, other than female descendants who marry, and their descendants, shall bear the name of Windsor.' In 1960, it was announced that future descendants would bear the surname Mountbatten-Windsor.

Following the death of King George V, in 1936, the royal succession itself was straightforward within the House of Windsor, except for the abdication of King Edward VIII (r.January–December 1936) later that year.

The crisis soon passed, and the Duke of York succeeded as King George VI (r.1936–52), ably supported by his wife,

Queen Elizabeth (1900–2002), who was born Elizabeth Bowes Lyon and was the daughter of the Earl of Strathmore (1855–1944).

King George VI reigned through the Second World War. He lived to see his daughter, Princess Elizabeth, married, in 1947, to Prince Philip of Greece and Denmark (b.1921), by then Lieutenant Philip Mountbatten, RN, and the birth of two grandchildren, Prince Charles (b.1948) and Princess Anne (b.1950).

King George VI was succeeded by the present Sovereign, Queen Elizabeth II (r.1952–), who celebrates the Diamond Jubilee of her reign in 2012. Her husband, Prince Philip, is also a descendant of Queen Victoria (see Ancestry of HRH The Duke of Edinburgh, page 62).

Following Queen Elizabeth II, the line of succession is secure. Her son, Charles, Prince of Wales, married in 1981; his first wife, Diana, Princess of Wales (1961–97), was herself a descendant of the Stuart kings. They had two sons, Prince William (b.1982) and Prince Henry (b.1984).

BELOW
Sir Herbert James Gunn (1893–1964), *Elizabeth II*, 1953–4. The Queen is depicted in her coronation dress and robes. Many copies were made of this portrait, to hang in British embassies around the world.

House of Windsor

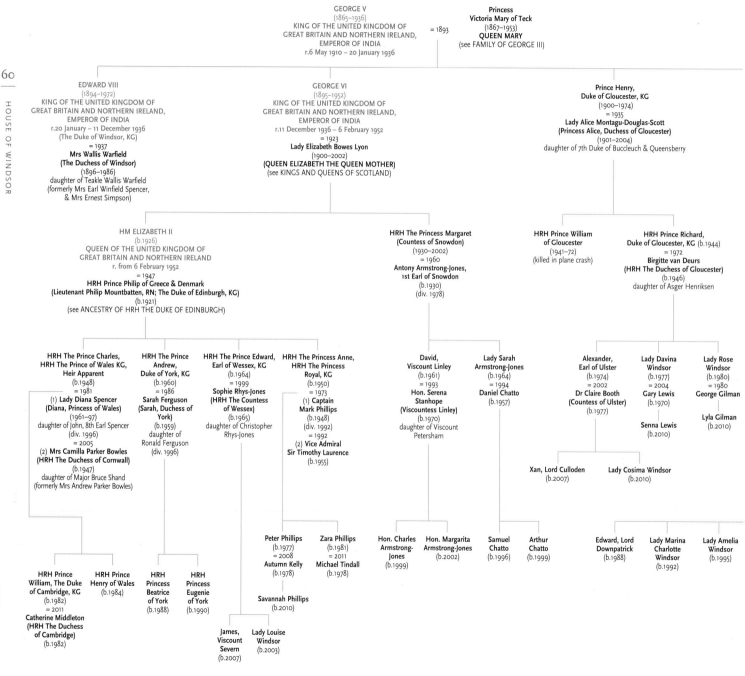

GEORGE V
(1865–1936)
KING OF THE UNITED KINGDOM OF
GREAT BRITAIN AND NORTHERN IRELAND,
EMPEROR OF INDIA
r.6 May 1910 – 20 January 1936

= 1893

**Princess
Victoria Mary of Teck**
(1867–1953)
QUEEN MARY
(SEE FAMILY OF GEORGE III)

EDWARD VIII
(1894–1972)
KING OF THE UNITED KINGDOM OF
GREAT BRITAIN AND NORTHERN IRELAND,
EMPEROR OF INDIA
r.20 January – 11 December 1936
(The Duke of Windsor, KG)
= 1937
**Mrs Wallis Warfield
(The Duchess of Windsor)**
(1896–1986)
daughter of Teakle Wallis Warfield
(formerly Mrs Earl Winfield Spencer,
& Mrs Ernest Simpson)

GEORGE VI
(1895–1952)
KING OF THE UNITED KINGDOM OF
GREAT BRITAIN AND NORTHERN IRELAND,
EMPEROR OF INDIA
r.11 December 1936 – 6 February 1952
= 1923
Lady Elizabeth Bowes Lyon
(1900–2002)
(QUEEN ELIZABETH THE QUEEN MOTHER)
(see KINGS AND QUEENS OF SCOTLAND)

**Prince Henry,
Duke of Gloucester, KG**
(1900–1974)
= 1935
**Lady Alice Montagu-Douglas-Scott
(Princess Alice, Duchess of Gloucester)**
(1901–2004)
daughter of 7th Duke of Buccleuch & Queensberry

HM ELIZABETH II
(b.1926)
QUEEN OF THE UNITED KINGDOM OF
GREAT BRITAIN AND NORTHERN IRELAND
r. from 6 February 1952
= 1947
HRH Prince Philip of Greece & Denmark
(Lieutenant Philip Mountbatten, RN; The Duke of Edinburgh, KG)
(b.1921)
(see ANCESTRY OF HRH THE DUKE OF EDINBURGH)

**HRH The Princess Margaret
(Countess of Snowdon)**
(1930–2002)
= 1960
**Antony Armstrong-Jones,
1st Earl of Snowdon**
(b.1930)
(div. 1978)

**HRH Prince William
of Gloucester**
(1941–72)
(killed in plane crash)

**HRH Prince Richard,
Duke of Gloucester, KG** (b.1944)
= 1972
**Birgitte van Deurs
(HRH The Duchess of Gloucester)**
(b.1946)
daughter of Asger Henriksen

**HRH The Prince Charles,
HRH The Prince of Wales KG,
Heir Apparent**
(b.1948)
= 1981
(1) **Lady Diana Spencer**
(Diana, Princess of Wales)
(1961–97)
daughter of John, 8th Earl Spencer
(div. 1996)
= 2005
(2) **Mrs Camilla Parker Bowles**
(HRH The Duchess of Cornwall)
(b.1947)
daughter of Major Bruce Shand
(formerly Mrs Andrew Parker Bowles)

**HRH The Prince
Andrew,
Duke of York, KG**
(b.1960)
= 1986
**Sarah Ferguson
(Sarah, Duchess of
York)**
(b.1959)
daughter of
Ronald Ferguson
(div. 1996)

**HRH The Prince Edward,
Earl of Wessex, KG**
(b.1964)
= 1999
**Sophie Rhys-Jones
(HRH The Countess
of Wessex)**
(b.1965)
daughter of Christopher
Rhys-Jones

**HRH The Princess Anne,
HRH The Princess
Royal, KG**
(b.1950)
= 1973
(1) **Captain
Mark Phillips**
(b.1948)
(div. 1992)
= 1992
(2) **Vice Admiral
Sir Timothy Laurence**
(b.1955)

**David,
Viscount Linley**
(b.1961)
= 1993
**Hon. Serena
Stanhope
(Viscountess Linley)**
(b.1970)
daughter of Viscount
Petersham

**Lady Sarah
Armstrong-Jones**
(b.1964)
= 1994
Daniel Chatto
(b.1957)

**Alexander,
Earl of Ulster**
(b.1974)
= 2002
**Dr Claire Booth
(Countess of Ulster)**
(b.1977)

**Lady Davina
Windsor**
(b.1977)
= 2004
Gary Lewis
(b.1970)

**Lady Rose
Windsor**
(b.1980)
= 1980
George Gilman

**HRH Prince
William, The Duke
of Cambridge, KG**
(b.1982)
= 2011
**Catherine Middleton
(HRH The Duchess
of Cambridge)**
(b.1982)

**HRH Prince
Henry of Wales**
(b.1984)

**HRH
Princess Beatrice
of York**
(b.1988)

**HRH
Princess
Eugenie
of York**
(b.1990)

Peter Phillips
(b.1977)
= 2008
Autumn Kelly
(b.1978)

Zara Phillips
(b.1981)
= 2011
Michael Tindall
(b.1978)

**Hon. Charles
Armstrong-
Jones**
(b.1999)

**Hon. Margarita
Armstrong-Jones**
(b.2002)

**Samuel
Chatto**
(b.1996)

**Arthur
Chatto**
(b.1999)

Xan, Lord Culloden
(b.2007)

Lady Cosima Windsor
(b.2010)

Senna Lewis
(b.2010)

Lyla Gilman
(b.2010)

**Edward, Lord
Downpatrick**
(b.1988)

**Lady Marina
Charlotte
Windsor**
(b.1992)

**Lady Amelia
Windsor**
(b.1995)

Savannah Phillips
(b.2010)

**James,
Viscount
Severn**
(b.2007)

**Lady Louise
Windsor**
(b.2003)

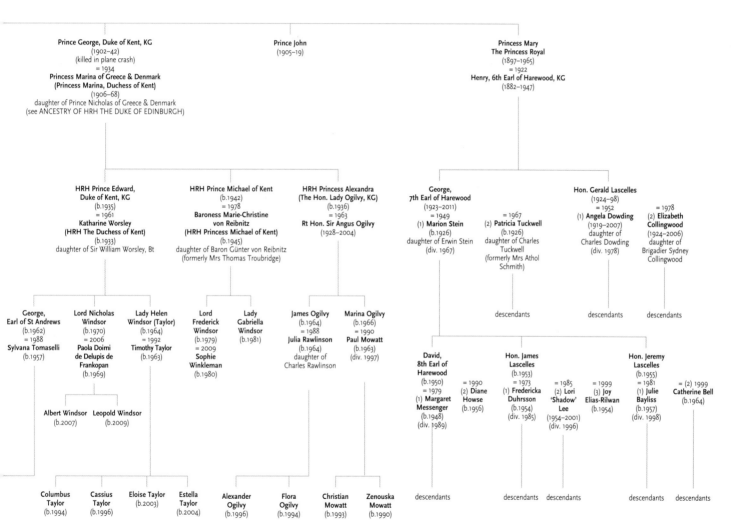

Prince George, Duke of Kent, KG
(1902–42)
(killed in plane crash)
= 1934
Princess Marina of Greece & Denmark
(Princess Marina, Duchess of Kent)
(1906–68)
daughter of Prince Nicholas of Greece & Denmark
(see ANCESTRY OF HRH THE DUKE OF EDINBURGH)

Prince John
(1905–19)

Princess Mary
The Princess Royal
(1897–1965)
= 1922
Henry, 6th Earl of Harewood, KG
(1882–1947)

HRH Prince Edward,
Duke of Kent, KG
(b.1935)
= 1961
Katharine Worsley
(HRH The Duchess of Kent)
(b.1933)
daughter of Sir William Worsley, Bt

HRH Prince Michael of Kent
(b.1942)
= 1978
Baroness Marie-Christine
von Reibnitz
(HRH Princess Michael of Kent)
(b.1945)
daughter of Baron Günter von Reibnitz
(formerly Mrs Thomas Troubridge)

HRH Princess Alexandra
(The Hon. Lady Ogilvy, KG)
(b.1936)
= 1963
Rt Hon. Sir Angus Ogilvy
(1928–2004)

George,
7th Earl of Harewood
(1923–2011)
= 1949
(1) Marion Stein
(b.1926)
daughter of Erwin Stein
(div. 1967)

= 1967
(2) Patricia Tuckwell
(b.1926)
daughter of Charles
Tuckwell
(formerly Mrs Athol
Schmith)

Hon. Gerald Lascelles
(1924–98)
= 1952
(1) Angela Dowding
(1919–2007)
daughter of
Charles Dowding
(div. 1978)

= 1978
(2) Elizabeth
Collingwood
(1924–2006)
daughter of
Brigadier Sydney
Collingwood

George,
Earl of St Andrews
(b.1962)
= 1988
Sylvana Tomaselli
(b.1957)

Lord Nicholas
Windsor
(b.1970)
= 2006
Paola Doimi
de Delupis de
Frankopan
(b.1969)

Lady Helen
Windsor (Taylor)
(b.1964)
= 1992
Timothy Taylor
(b.1963)

Lord
Frederick
Windsor
(b.1979)
= 2009
Sophie
Winkleman
(b.1980)

Lady
Gabriella
Windsor
(b.1981)

James Ogilvy
(b.1964)
= 1988
Julia Rawlinson
(b.1964)
daughter of
Charles Rawlinson

Marina Ogilvy
(b.1966)
= 1990
Paul Mowatt
(b.1963)
(div. 1997)

descendants

descendants

descendants

Albert Windsor
(b.2007)

Leopold Windsor
(b.2009)

David,
8th Earl of
Harewood
(b.1950)
= 1979
(1) Margaret
Messenger
(b.1948)
(div. 1989)

= 1990
(2) Diane
Howse
(b.1956)

Hon. James
Lascelles
(b.1953)
= 1973
(1) Fredericka
Duhrsson
(b.1954)
(div. 1985)

= 1985
(2) Lori
'Shadow'
Lee
(1954–2001)
(div. 1996)

= 1999
(3) Joy
Elias-Rilwan
(b.1954)

Hon. Jeremy
Lascelles
(b.1955)
= 1981
(1) Julie
Bayliss
(b.1957)
(div. 1998)

= (2) 1999
Catherine Bell
(b.1964)

Columbus
Taylor
(b.1994)

Cassius
Taylor
(b.1996)

Eloise Taylor
(b.2003)

Estella
Taylor
(b.2004)

Alexander
Ogilvy
(b.1996)

Flora
Ogilvy
(b.1994)

Christian
Mowatt
(b.1993)

Zenouska
Mowatt
(b.1990)

descendants

descendants

descendants

descendants

descendants

Ancestry of HRH The Duke of Edinburgh

This family tree shows select members of the family of HRH Prince Philip, The Duke of Edinburgh. Both Queen Alexandra and The Duke of Edinburgh descend from King Christian IX of Denmark (1818–1906). One can also trace the descent of Prince Philip from the Houses of Hesse-Darmstadt and Battenberg, and thus through his great-grandmother, Alice, Grand Duchess of Hesse, daughter of Queen Victoria. A number of kings and queens of Europe are included on this tree to show how The Duke of Edinburgh is related to Queen Margrethe II of Denmark (b.1940), King Juan Carlos of Spain (b.1938), King Michael of Romania (b.1921) and King Constantine II of Greece (b.1940). It includes his uncle (by marriage), the late King Gustaf VI Adolf of Sweden (1882–1973), and his great-aunt, Princess Alix of Hesse, the last Empress of Russia (1872–1918).

OPPOSITE

David Poole (b.1931), *The Duke of Edinburgh*, 1986. This is one of a set of three portraits of The Duke painted by Poole.

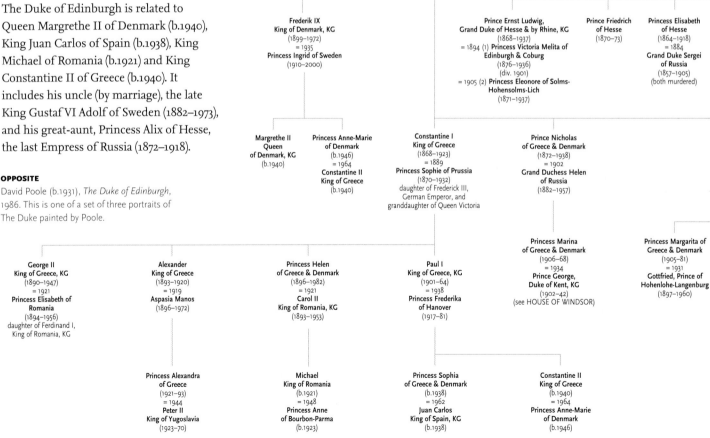

**Arms of HRH PRINCE PHILIP,
THE DUKE OF EDINBURGH**

Ludwig II,
Grand Duke of Hesse
(1777–1848) = 1804 Princess
Wilhelmine of Baden
(1788–1836)

Ludwig III,
Grand Duke of Hesse
(1806–77)

Prince Charles of Hesse
(1809–77)
= 1836
Princess Elisabeth of Prussia
(1815–85)
daughter of Prince Wilhelm of Prussia

Grand Duke Alexander of Hesse
(1823–88)
= 1851
Julie von Haucke
(1825–95)

Princess Marie
of Hesse
(1824–80)
= 1841
Emperor Alexander II
of Russia, KG
(1818–81)
(father of Emperor Alexander III
of Russia)

Ludwig IV,
Grand Duke of Hesse & by Rhine, KG
(1837–92)
= 1861 (1) Princess Alice
(Grand Duchess of Hesse & by Rhine)
(1843–78)
daughter of Queen Victoria

= 1884 (2) Madame
Alexandrine Kolémine
(1854–1941)
(m. annulled 1884)

Princess Irene
of Hesse
(1866–1953)
= 1888
Prince Henry
of Prussia, KG
(1862–1929)

Princess Alix
of Hesse
(Empress (Tsarina) Alexandra
Feodorovna)
(1872–1918)
= 1894
Emperor (Tsar) Nicholas II
of Russia, KG
(1868–1918)
(both murdered)

Princess Marie
of Hesse
(1874–8)

Princess Victoria of
Hesse
(1863–1950) = 1884

Prince Louis
of Battenberg
(1854–1921)
(later Admiral of the
Fleet, 1st Marquess of
Milford Haven)

Prince Henry of Battenberg,
KG
(1858–96)
= 1885
The Princess Beatrice
(1857–1944)
daughter of Queen Victoria

Prince Andrew
of Greece & Denmark
(1882–1944) = 1903

Princess Alice
of Battenberg
(1885–1969)

Lady Louise Mountbatten
(1889–1965)
= 1923
Gustaf VI Adolf
King of Sweden, KG
(1882–1973)

George, 2nd Marquess
of Milford Haven
(1892–1938)
= 1916
Countess Nada de Torby
(1896–1963)

Louis, Admiral of the Fleet,
Earl Mountbatten of Burma, KG
(1900–1979)
= 1922
Hon. Edwina Ashley
(1901–60)

Princess Victoria Eugénie of
Battenberg
(1887–1969)
= 1906
Alfonso XIII
King of Spain, KG
(1886–1941)

Princess Theodora of
Greece & Denmark
(1906–69)
= 1931
Berthold,
Margrave of Baden
(1906–63)

Princess Cecilia
of Greece & Denmark
(1911–37)
= 1931
Prince Georg
Donatus, Hereditary
Grand Duke of Hesse
(1906–37)

Princess Sophia
of Greece & Denmark
(1914–2001)
= 1930
(1) Prince Christoph
of Hesse-Cassel
(1901–43)
= 1946
(2) Prince
Georg Wilhelm
of Hanover
(1915–2006)

HRH Prince Philip of
Greece & Denmark
(Lieutenant Philip Mountbatten, RN;
HRH The Duke of Edinburgh, KG)
(b.1921)
= 1947
HM ELIZABETH II
(b.1926)
QUEEN OF THE UNITED
KINGDOM OF GREAT BRITAIN
AND NORTHERN IRELAND
(see HOUSE OF WINDSOR)

Patricia, 2nd Countess
Mountbatten of Burma
(b.1924)
= 1946
John, 7th Lord Brabourne
(1924–2005)

Lady Pamela Mountbatten
(b.1929)
= 1960
David Hicks
(1929–98)

Infante Juan,
Count of Barcelona
(1913–93)
=
Infanta Maria
de las Mercedes,
of the Two Sicilies
(1910–2000)

Juan Carlos
King of Spain, KG
(b.1938)
= 1962
Princess Sophia
of Greece & Denmark
(b.1938)

ABOVE
Her Majesty The Queen
and members of the Royal
Family watch a fly-past
from the balcony of
Buckingham Palace after
the ceremony of Trooping
the Colour in June 2011,
to celebrate The Queen's
official birthday.